Get Your *kids fit*

The parents' guide to healthy, happy, active kids

KELLY HOLMES

With Eileen Fursland

700
D0432964

Acknowledgements

The publisher would like to thank the following for their invaluable help in the production of this book: David Haskins and Louise Wolsey at the Youth Sport Trust; Jane Cowmeadow; and Adam Lawrence for the photography. Dame Kelly Holmes would like to thank everyone who has contributed to the contents and production of the book.

First published in Great Britain in 2007 by
Virgin Books Ltd
Thames Wharf Studios
Rainville Road
London
W6 9HA

Copyright © Kelly Holmes with Eileen Fursland 2007

WORCESTERSHIRE COUNTY COUNCIL	
748	
Bertrams	18.07.07
613.7042	£14.99
WL	

The right of Kelly Holmes with Eileen Fursland to be identified as the Authors of this work has been asserted by them in accordance with the Copyright, Designs and Patents Act, 1988.

This book is sold subject to the condition that it shall not, by way of trade or otherwise, be lent, resold, hired out or otherwise circulated without the publisher's prior written consent in any form of binding or cover other than that in which it is published and without a similar condition including this condition being imposed on the subsequent purchaser.

A catalogue record for this book is available from the British Library.

ISBN 978 0 7535 1265 4

The paper used in this book is a natural, recyclable product made from wood grown in sustainable forests. The manufacturing process conforms to the regulations of the country of origin.

Designed by Virgin Books Ltd

Printed and bound in Germany

While every effort has been made to ensure the information contained in this book is accurate, it is advisory only and should not be used as an alternative to seeking specialist medical advice. Neither the authors nor the publisher will be held responsible for any personal injury or other damage or loss arising from the use or misuse of the information in this book.

Picture credits
All photography of Kelly Holmes and kids © Adam Lawrence/Virgin Books Ltd, except on the following pages: 24, 31, 33, 39, 41, 74, 75, 77, 81, 93, 109, 116, 121 © Shutterstock; 26, 45, 47, 60, 70, 94, 106, 111, 112, 117, 118, 131 © Corbis; 13, 27, 113, 114, 119 © Getty Images; 37(bottom), 40, 123 © Alamy.

All illustrations © Andrew Roberts, except those on pages 16–21 © Derek Lawrie/Vertigo Creative Ltd.

Contents

Introduction

Congratulations! By picking up this book you've decided that you want to do something really positive for your kids. By helping them to get active and healthy, you'll not only be helping them now, but you'll also be giving them the best chance in life to grow up to be healthy and happy individuals.

Children have a lot to distract them nowadays – far more than I did when I was young – but there's absolutely no excuse for kids to be stuck indoors in front of the TV or computer screen for hours on end. There are hundreds of fun activities out there – something for everyone, of every age, ability or level of fitness – and this book is bursting with great ideas.

You'll find lots of fun games for youngsters, which will get them out of the house and exercising without them even knowing it! Schools are making really good progress in getting all children more active through their PE and sports initiatives, but there are plenty of other ways of introducing activity into your child's everyday routine, from walking to school to playground games.

And what about older kids? It's true that many teenagers – particularly girls – can lose interest in sport. But I'll give you plenty of ideas to keep them motivated and to find that one activity that will make a difference to their lives.

As National School Sport Champion, I have dedicated myself to helping improve the fitness of our children, and I am truly passionate about inspiring kids through education, sport and activities.

But parents can make the real difference, and it's up to you to motivate your children to try something new and to get out there and start enjoying all the opportunities available to them.

And that's where this book comes in – to help you get your kids off the sofa, out of the house and into the habit of regular activity.

Chapter 1

Giving your kids a healthy start in life

I firmly believe that if you teach your kids good habits and encourage them to get involved in physical activity at a young age, you can really boost their confidence and self-esteem. If your children participate in activity and eat healthily they'll have a much better chance of being fit and healthy for the rest of their life.

What's more, if your kids are more active and get involved in sport, outdoor activities or dance they'll have more fun – childhood shouldn't be all about sitting in front of a TV or computer screen!

With so much emphasis on and discussion about the state of children's fitness today, I believe parents have a huge amount of responsibility for keeping their kids active.

Being physically active can help your child:
- Have a healthy heart
- Develop strong muscles and bones
- Stay a healthy weight
- Relax and cope with stress
- Enjoy mixing with others
- Feel a sense of achievement
- Concentrate better in school
- Gain more confidence
- Have higher self-esteem

Parents can make a difference

Schools are getting much better at providing PE, sport and physical activity for children and young people, but schools can't do it all – they don't have time in the curriculum to provide all the activity a child needs, so kids need to be active at home too. And that means it's up to you to give them opportunities and encourage them to be active.

How much activity do children need?

Your kids should aim to participate in activity of at least moderate intensity for one hour every day. If they don't do much activity at the moment they should start by doing at least half an hour per day. This could be brisk walking, active play, cycling, swimming, dance or most sports. The one hour doesn't have to be done all at once – it can be done in mixed active play in shorter bursts throughout the day. At least twice a week, children should take part in some activities that help to enhance and maintain muscular strength and flexibility and bone strength. This could include climbing, skipping, jumping or gymnastics, and for older children dance, aerobics and sports such as basketball.

Do you need to do more to get your kids on the go?

Get kids on the go! is a booklet from the British Heart Foundation.

Here's a quick quiz from the BHF to help you decide if your child is doing enough activity outside school PE lessons:

Does your child watch less than three and a half hours of television each day?	Yes	No
Does your child walk or cycle to school?	Yes	No
Does your child play outside most days?	Yes	No
Does your child take part in organised sport or recreational activities, either at school, at after-school clubs or outside school?	Yes	No
Do you take part in activity as a family (e.g. walking, swimming or playing active games?)	Yes	No

All YES answers
It's likely that your child is already participating in enough activity outside school. Encourage them to keep up the good work!

All NO answers
Your child is almost certainly not doing enough activity outside school. You need to encourage them to do more, building up their activity levels gradually. Don't expect them to make big changes overnight!

A mixture of YES and NO answers
Your child may not be enjoying all the benefits that an active lifestyle brings. If they are not doing thirty to sixty minutes of activity on most days, think about ways they could do more.

You can send for a free copy of the BHF booklet at the address on page 143

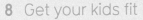

Television just encourages kids to lounge around for hours – often snacking at the same time. Get tough – limit the number of hours your kids are allowed to watch the telly!

Physical activity can be fun!

The Kelly Holmes School Challenge involved 25 different Kent schools, including my own old school, Hugh Christie in Tonbridge.

I would turn up at the schools with all the equipment that my dad and granddad had helped me collect – tyres and planks painted in bright colours that were used as part of a mini-assault course. There was also a supermarket shopping trolley for the 'Trolley Push', in which someone would be pushed down to one end of the hall where there were apples in water and sweets buried in flour. After they'd struggled to take a bite of the apple, they had to get a sweet with their teeth.

They got into a fantastic mess and loved every minute. The teachers would say to me, 'We hardly ever see them running around like this, having so much fun. For once, they are not moaning!' The days were great successes with the children and I kept the school challenge going for three years.

Finding the time

Doing regular physical activity with your kids and taking them to after-school classes or sports clubs can sometimes be difficult when you have so many other demands on your time. Sharing things like this with other families works well – taking turns and helping each other out means parents have a lighter load.

Often, having friends to play with can encourage kids to be more active – especially if you provide some basic equipment, like balls, racquets, bats and basketball hoops and let them get on with it. Activities like roller-skating and cycling are more fun with friends.

Encourage them to play outdoors, making dens or kicking a football around with their friends. It's good for their independence and makes them more resourceful and less likely to complain of being bored.

Your support does matter!

Parents are role models for their kids. Your child will take on board your enthusiasm (or lack of it!). It takes a very individual child to go against what the rest of the family does.

As many parents have discovered, sport can be a really positive and important part in their child's life – and your attitude can make all the difference for your child.

'Although there is always a great deal of criticism of overenthusiastic parents/carers who shout abuse and behave badly on the sidelines, those who don't encourage and support their children's involvement in sport are a much greater hindrance to long–term participation. Children whose parents/carers actively encourage and support their involvement in sport are more likely to value and enjoy it.'

How to Coach Children in Sport, sports coach UK

Mad about sport?

Sports-mad kids will love the CBBC website: it's got interviews with sports stars – in everything from wheelchair basketball to camogie and ski racing – message boards, tricks, a sporting-events calendar and lots more.

See www.bbc.co.uk/cbbc/sport for more details.

If you do want to make some changes, the rest of this book will help you. And the whole family could end up healthier and fitter!

If your child is disabled

Physical activity is important for every child – perhaps even more so for young disabled people. It helps to focus on the things your child can do and to think carefully about the ways they can be included. To help with this, experts who work with young disabled people have devised the inclusion spectrum.

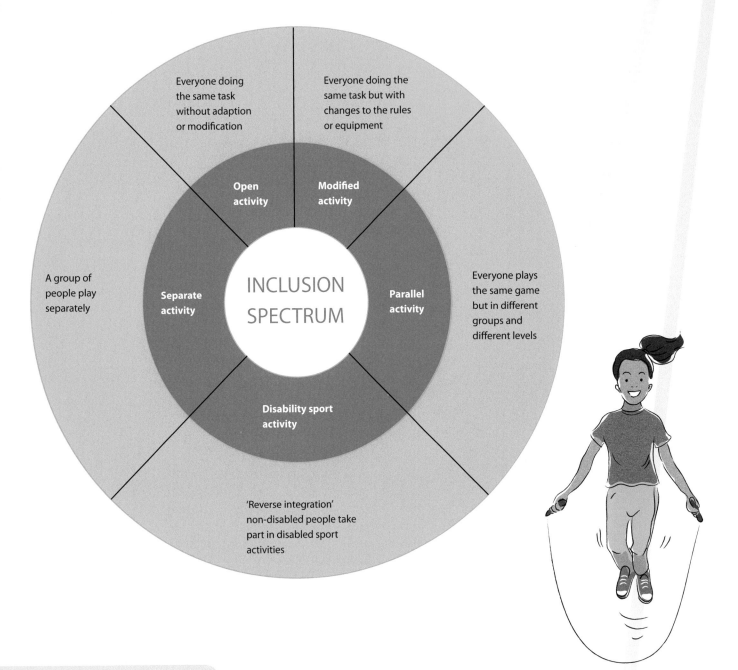

Everyone doing the same task without adaption or modification

Everyone doing the same task but with changes to the rules or equipment

Open activity

Modified activity

A group of people play separately

Separate activity

INCLUSION SPECTRUM

Parallel activity

Everyone plays the same game but in different groups and different levels

Disability sport activity

'Reverse integration' non-disabled people take part in disabled sport activities

Some children may enjoy separation in some activities but have the ability and motivation to join in open activity at other times. The inclusion spectrum gives parents of young disabled people a chance to consider carefully how their children can gain the most from physical activity.

Once the type of activity has been chosen it is important that everyone understands the best way for individuals to take part. A discussion with everyone before an activity starts is essential and often a great way to start a game because then everyone understands each other.

Many sports are keen to include young disabled people. If you want your child to take part in an organised activity or sport, talk to the leader or coach about your child's needs and abilities and work out how they can take part.

The Youth Sport Trust has a range of excellent resources on group games and physical activities for children and young people, with information on how each one can be adapted for young disabled people.

Contact Youth Sport Trust, details on page 142.

Disability sports organisations can also help – details on page 143.

Chapter 2

Having fun – Games and activities for young kids

Children should be allowed to be children and, most importantly, to have fun! I really believe that if you play games with your kids and give them the opportunity to try a variety of different activities then they'll be happier and healthier individuals.

This chapter is packed with lots of fun games and activities, for kids aged four or five to ten or eleven, which I guarantee will get your kids off the sofa, out of the house and having the time of their life.

Getting your kids outdoors

When I was young, I used to play outside a lot. My friends and I used to hang around in the park and pass the time playing hopscotch, football, skipping games or tag.

The best thing was going down to the brook – we were allowed to play in the woods down there for hours at a time. We'd make rafts out of broken logs and paddle down the stream, pretending we were pirates or explorers. We used our imagination. I think lots of kids don't get the chance to do enough of that kind of play these days.

Wide-open spaces and natural places are really great for kids. They can run as fast and as far as they like, explore and get wet and dirty. In a park, a wood or on a beach, kids feel more independent, free from adult agendas and they can explore their own ideas, constructing their own little worlds. Their creativity and imagination can really kick in. They can test themselves and their nerve, climbing trees, rolling down hills or jumping stepping stones.

Many kids prefer this kind of natural adventure play to formal sports. And there are ways to do it safely – even if it means keeping an eye on them from a distance.

Go walkies

Dogs were an important part of our family – we always had a dog and I love them. If your child isn't enthusiastic about going for a walk with you, see if you can beg, borrow or steal a neighbour's dog for an hour. It could make a walk a much more exciting prospect!

Outdoor games for kids

The Alphabet Game

Call out a letter of the alphabet and see if your kids can make the shape of the letter. When they have mastered this, try a game of Body Semaphore. In partners or small groups, the children make the shapes of letters to send a message to their friends.

Encourage your children to:
- Form the shapes of each letter of the alphabet. Are some letters more easy/difficult to make in terms of keeping their balance?
- Move with their eyes closed. Is it easier or more difficult to balance?
- Put a sequence of moves together. Can they do it to music?

Human Skittles

Get your kids to stand on one leg in a row, one metre apart. One person then rolls a ball towards them. The others must jump to avoid being hit by the ball.

The kids can take it in turns to roll the ball.

Encourage your children to:

- Try using different types of ball
- Make bigger or smaller jumps
- Flex their legs to absorb the landing

Lose Three Balls

Each child has a Hula Hoop and places it on the ground with three balls inside. They then have to move their balls one by one from their hoop into the other players' hoops. The winner is the one who gets rid of all their balls and stands in their hoop before anyone can put another ball in it.

Reach Out

Set out different circular layouts on the ground, like in the picture. Your child has to stand on one foot and touch with the other foot whichever marker you call out. For example, if you lay your markers in a clock layout, you can shout out a time (nine o'clock, say) and your child has to touch the marker that is in that position on a clock face.

Encourage your children to:
- Move the markers further apart
- Try doing it with a blindfold on

Jump the Stream

Place two ropes or lines on the ground to make the stream. You can make stepping stones with mats or with chalked/taped markers. Your kids have to try and jump over the stream without falling in.

Try varying the width of the stream to make it harder.

5

Floor Football

Mark out the football pitch as in the picture. The two players lie on their front facing each other. The object of the game is to get the ball past your opponent to score a goal. The ball must be on the ground when it passes the line.

Try making it harder with a blindfold!

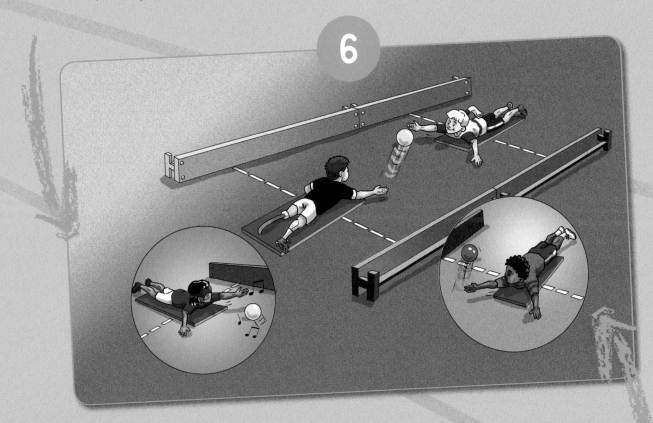

Other Games

Hopscotch

Draw a grid on the floor with a piece of chalk, like in the diagram. Toss a marker – a stone or a bottle top – into the first square. If the marker lands in the wrong square, you miss a turn.

If the marker goes in the right place, hop through the court, beginning on square one. You hop single squares on one foot and on side-by-side squares you land on two feet, with your left foot in the left square and your right foot in the right square. You can start hopping on either foot. However, you skip the square with the stone in it – hop right over.

When you reach the end of the court, turn around and hop back through the court, going back the other way and stopping to pick up the marker on the way back. This time you hop in the square where you left your marker. When you have finished the sequence, you continue your turn by throwing the marker into square number two, and repeating the pattern.

If at any time you step on a line, miss a square or lose your balance, your turn is over. Players begin their turns where they last left off. The winner is the first one who can complete the course for every numbered square.

Cops and Robbers/Cats and Mice

For this you need two teams with any number of players in each. All you need is plenty of open space to run around and a place that serves as the jail or cage. This could be a special corner of the playground, a bench, a tree, etc.

The team doing the chasing has to catch as many members of the other team as they can. When they catch someone, that person is their prisoner and they bring them back to the jail. The prisoner has to stay there until the end of the game (unless a fellow team member releases them).

The team that is being chased tries to free fellow team members who have been captured. They do this by making a run for the jail (while avoiding being caught themselves). If they make it to the jail, they release the prisoners, who can then scatter . . . and the game starts all over again.

Giants, wizards, elves

This is a game that works brilliantly with groups of kids of all ages – in fact, adults can have a lot of fun with it too! It's a variation on 'scissors, stone, paper', but instead of scissors, stone and paper, there are giants, wizards and elves:

- Wizards can beat elves, because of their greater magic powers
- Elves can beat giants, because they are small and can trip them up
- Giants can beat wizards, because of their huge size.

To start each round of the game, two teams each go into a huddle and decide whether their team will be giants, wizards or elves. Whichever they choose, they will need to remember the appropriate pose to adopt at the right moment:

- Wizards put hands above their heads in a 'pointy hat' shape
- Giants stand on tiptoes and stretch their arms up, making themselves as tall as possible
- Elves crouch down small

Then the two teams face each other, in two lines, a few metres apart. Someone says, 'One, two, three . . . NOW!' and all the members of the team adopt the appropriate pose for their chosen character.

The opposing team adopts their pose at the same time, and that's when the fun really starts.

- If one team are wizards and the other are giants, the giants chase after the wizards and try to catch them
- If one team are elves and the other are wizards, the wizards chase after the elves and try to catch them
- If one team are elves and the other giants, the elves chase the giants

The 'chasing' team catch as many members of the other team as they can. Each team has a 'safe' area several metres behind them and if they make it back there, they are home and can't be caught. But everyone who gets caught before they manage to reach home has to join the opposing team. Then you start the next round.

Mini-assault course

Make a mini-assault course or fitness circuit in the garden to get your kids active. You just need a bit of ingenuity. Have five or six 'stations', each with a different activity. Here are a few ideas.

- Jumping in and out of a hoop on the grass (or a circle drawn on the paving) ten times
- Climbing – up a tree, if there is one, or over something sturdy like a low wall
- Balancing – along a low bench, or walking in a perfectly straight line along a rope on the ground
- Scrambling through a 'tunnel' – if you open up both ends of those huge cardboard boxes that white goods come in, you've got your tunnel (or you could spread an old bedspread on the ground and get your child to wriggle underneath it and come out the other side)
- Running up and down the steps five times (or twenty, depending on how many steps you have and how much energy your child has!)
- Skipping with a skipping rope
- Bouncing a ball ten times on the ground or throwing it against a wall and catching it
- Aiming a ball into a bucket – can you get it in the bucket five times in a row?

Try a new activity

The British Heart Foundation has a great *Pocket Play Pack* aimed at kids from seven to eleven, to encourage children to become more active over a six-week period.

Keeping a record of how much time they spend on active games and playing is a great motivator. Your child can keep a record by colouring in segments on a 'stopwatch' on a colourful set of charts. They can show how long they have spent on various kinds of activities such as:

- **Walking – e.g. playing follow my leader, walking to school**
- **Running – e.g. playing chase, tennis, orienteering**
- **Wheels – e.g. skateboarding, scooting, roller-skating**
- **Dancing – e.g. break dancing, bhangra dancing, Hula Hoop**
- **Jumping – e.g. skipping, playing on a bouncy castle**

Kids add up each week's total and this motivates them to increase their total time each week. At the end, they can send off for a certificate to show how well they've done!

You can order a *Pocket Play Pack* free from the BHF (see page 143).

Kelly's challenge for kids

- Teach your parents or carers a game you play at school. Can they do it?

- Ask your parent or carer when they could take you for a bike ride. If they are busy, think of something you could do to save them a bit of time, like helping with the washing up or making your own sandwiches in the mornings. Then they might manage it!

- Ever tried hopscotch? Ask your parents or carers to show you how it's done – can they remember playing it when they were at school? If not the instructions are on page 22.

Kelly's family challenge

- Build some active family fun into your week – go out to the park, or for a swim, or for a bike ride together once or twice a week.

- Get together with another family – go to the park and play a football match against them. Each weekend, keep a tally of who wins – and every six weeks, the losing family has to cook Sunday lunch for everyone!

Make a chart

Help your child choose a skill to learn, like riding a bike or swimming, or an activity they want to get better at. Get them to illustrate or decorate a chart, like the one below, and fill it in to keep a record of how well they are doing.

Trying to improve on your previous performance is a big incentive for a child. For example, if they are learning to swim or ride their bike, you could record how far they manage to go each time, and encourage them to go a bit further every time.

what I want to get better swimming	How well am I doing?
Session 1	I swam 3 lengths of the pool
Session 2	
Session 3	
Session 4	
Session 5	
Session 6	

Get your kids off the sofa!

Even if you can't go far afield, you can get your kids to be more active at home. Try these ideas:

- Rearrange the furniture so you can drape bedspreads over tables and chairs to make a den. Kids will surprise you with the imaginative ideas they come up with as they crawl in and out of the den – is it an underground cave, a deserted cottage or a secret hiding place where they are safe from the wicked witch?

- Buy or borrow a dance DVD or get one of those dance-mat games and wiggle and bounce in the privacy of your own living room.

- Get the kids to wash the car – they'll love the chance to mess around with water and sponges and it saves on the cost of going to the car wash.

- Look at the games your kids have got stashed away in the cupboard – are there any that will get them off the sofa, like Twister for instance?

- Clear as much space as you can in the middle of the floor and put some coasters down on the carpet around the room. Make up a game where you have to move around the room, but you can only move by stepping on the coasters – for instance, you could be pursuing your child through shark-infested waters and the coasters are the rocks where you are safe from the sharks.

- On rainy days, bring out some play equipment that will get your child moving – like a play tunnel and a trampoline – or just take all the cushions off the sofa and armchairs and make a mountain with them in the middle of the room for them to climb and jump on and roll off.

'Balls in the house? You must be joking!'

Playing with balls indoors doesn't have to be a complete no-no – try a larger, slower-moving ball like a large sponge ball or beach ball. Balloons pose even less risk to your valuables and give younger children plenty of reaction time. Games like skittles, in which you roll balls along the carpet, work well too.

Indoor games for young ones

Musical shapes

Play some lively music to get the kids bouncing around. When you stop the music, they have to freeze and hold the pose they are in – without wobbling or giggling – until you start the music again. Try making them laugh by pulling faces or giving them a gentle push on the back to see if they fall over!

Sleeping lions

This is similar, but when the music stops the kids have to fall on the floor, keep very still and pretend to be 'sleeping lions'. Any lion that moves, even a fraction, is 'out'.

Kelly's challenge for kids
How far can you jump?

- Mark out a distance on some grass by putting a line or some other marker at either end. See how many jumps it takes you to cover the distance.

- Now see if you can reduce the number of jumps you need to cover the same distance. If you can, it means your jumps are getting longer!

- Try taking a run-up – can you jump further?

Safety notes

- Children should try not to bend their knees more than 90 degrees when landing. They do need to bend their knees, of course, to absorb the impact – but repeatedly bending them too much can damage the knee ligaments.
- They should do this on a soft surface – grass is good, but not wet grass as that's too slippery.
- Trainers should be worn.

Out-of-school activities

I had lots of choices and opportunities when I was a child and tried all sorts of out-of-school clubs. If you give your kids the opportunity to choose what they want to do, then they can find the sport or activity that makes the difference to their life. They soon know if they like something or not. And if they're good at something, they keep at it. It's always exciting for kids to try something new, like trampolining or judo.

What's on offer depends on where you live, of course, but in most places there is a huge choice of out-of-school classes and clubs for kids. With luck, your child will discover something they enjoy and are good at, which could turn into a lifelong interest.

Starting young

Kids can start to learn things like ice-skating, horse-riding or gym from as young as four.

The Youth Sport Trust has produced Top Tots, a physical play programme for children from eighteen months to three years, which can be used in pre-schools, nurseries and by parents at home. There's a bag of safe, colourful equipment and educational resource cards (for more information see www.youthsporttrust.org/page/top-tots/index.html).

Lots of places have Tumble Tots gym classes for toddlers and pre-schoolers. In these classes, pre-schoolers learn to be with other children, take turns and listen to instructions, as well as developing their co-ordination, balance and physical confidence.

What to look for in an out-of-school class

- What are the club leader's or coach's qualifications and experience?
- How much will the class cost? And how much for all the kit, like ballet shoes, leotards and so on? What about further down the line – will there be ballet shows that you have to buy costumes for?
- How easy will it be for you to get there? If it's at an inconvenient time or the traffic is awful, you might end up missing a lot of sessions.
- Look for a good ratio of adult leaders to children – this means closer supervision and less waiting around for their turn.
- What are the facilities like for you if you have to wait there? You don't really want to have to sit on a hard chair for an hour in a cold corridor if there's any alternative!
- Make sure the club leaders have had a Criminal Records Bureau check (see page 133).
- Find out if it is competitive. Some children relish competition but others are put off by it.

Ask if your child can try the class a couple of times to make sure they like it before you spend money on a whole term's classes.

To find a good class in your local area:

- ○ Ask around among your friends and other parents in the playground
- ○ Search the Internet
- ○ Ask at your local leisure centre or library
- ○ Phone your local council or check its website
- ○ If there's a particular sport or activity your child is interested in, the national organisation for that activity may tell you what's available locally – there are contact details for some of these on page 142.

There's more information on finding sports clubs and coaching in Chapter 8.

Swimming

The swimming and water safety website at www.qca.org.uk/safeswimming has information on how teachers teach swimming at school. There is also a section for parents with some useful tips on increasing children's water confidence and teaching them to swim. Here are a few of the suggestions:

- Explain that arms and hands play an important part in helping us to move along in the water. Show your child how to pull and push underwater with their hands to make it ripple, whirl and surge. This is different from splashing, which is done on the surface.

- Encourage your child to take their feet off the ground. Provide a bit of support at first – they could hold on to the rail or the side of the pool, or you could hold them gently under the arms, back or tummy.

- With your child wearing armbands or a ring, get them to spin around in the water and to move backwards as well as forwards. Make it a game – you could pretend to be a 'shark' that they have to get away from!

- Try letting a little air out of their armbands or ring as they get more confident, to gradually reduce the amount of support provided.

- Practise different ways of kicking. Give them a large float or ring to hold on to and encourage them to stretch their arms out in front of them. See if they can splash the water with their feet and, later, make a little ripple on the surface of the water.

- Get your child to 'swim' for the first time by asking them to plunge towards you or the side of the pool. With encouragement, they will pluck up the courage to throw themselves forwards, take their legs off the ground and reach for you or the side with their hands stretched out.

- Explain that kicking your legs and pulling with your arms helps you to go further. Encourage them to keep their hands stretched out in front of them, slightly cupped.

- Show them how pulling their hands down the front or the side of their body propels them forward.

- Can they float? See if your child can keep their head above water by using their arms to make 'sculling' movements and kicking their legs.

If your child is disabled

There is a fantastic range of activities available for young disabled people. These include boccia, goalball, floor lacrosse, Tee Ball, Polybat, table cricket and table hockey.

All of these are featured in the Youth Sport Trust's sports ability programmes. Parents can prepare children for these games by helping them practise at home and involving them in all the activities suggested in this chapter.

Swimming can give a wonderful sense of freedom to children and young people who use a wheelchair or find walking difficult. For over fifty years, disabled people have been experiencing the freedom of water using special techniques known as the Halliwick Method. The Halliwick Association of Swimming Therapy has a national (and international) network of swimming clubs for children and adults with any kind of disability, including sensory disabilities. There are also competitions at local, regional, national and international levels, where swimmers compete. See www. halliwick.org.uk for more details.

Chapter 3
School life

I loved playing sport at school – it gave me a new lease of life and confidence with my classmates. But PE or games lessons are not the only way that your kids can build physical activity into their school life.

I used to cycle to school and back, three miles every day. It kept me fit and I enjoyed the freedom it gave me. Walking or cycling to school, and enjoying activities in the playground, are all simple ways of building more activity into your child's daily life.

Walk to school

Walking to school with your child, if you can manage it, is a great way of building some physical activity into their normal daily routine. It gets your kids off to a good start for the day, as they will be more alert when they arrive at school after a walk. It also teaches them that not every trip has to be in a car – they can use their legs to get them to places! And teachers say that walking to school makes children more receptive to learning.

Siobhan, a mum from Middlesex, says:

'I used to drive my little boy to school. It is about a ten-minute walk, but when I drove it could take twenty minutes, due to traffic and trying to find a parking space. Now we walk in whatever weather and it is a good way of having some quality time with your child. We can find out what he's been doing and it's very sociable. We now speak to and acknowledge other parents. We've got friendly with the lady with the dogs and we feel part of our community – it's also a good bit of exercise!'

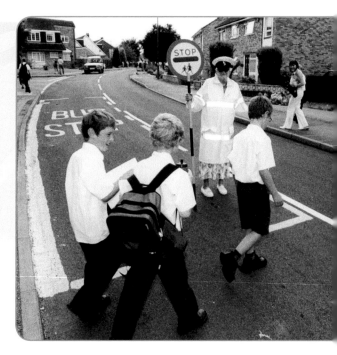

The 'Walk to School' campaign

More than half the nation's children still do not regularly walk to school and the number of cars doing the school run is increasing. Lots of schools see traffic congestion around the school gates as a real problem and want to combat it. 'Walk to School' is a campaign asking parents, pupils and teachers to walk to and from school whenever possible. Each year, there are two national 'Walk to School Weeks', which encourage everyone to try walking to school. Some schools offer incentives for pupils who walk to school (such as stickers or certificates) and teachers incorporate road safety or environmental awareness into lesson time.

And, once they get used to the idea, most kids soon discover that they actually enjoy walking to school with a parent or friends.

See www.walktoschool.org.uk for more information.

Other benefits of walking

Walking to school with your child will help them develop the skills they will eventually need to travel independently, so encourage them to take responsibility and they will learn lots about:

- Road safety – knowing where and when to cross
- Personal safety – knowing how to keep safe and what to do if approached by a stranger or bully
- Getting a better sense of their local area
- Planning a route and working out how long journeys are likely to take
- Dressing suitably for the weather

Kelly's challenge for kids

- Learn the Green Cross Code. When you are walking to school with an adult, show them that you understand the Code by talking them through it when you need to cross roads together.

- Talk about safe places to cross the road and the kind of things you need to look out for.

- As you walk to school with your parent or carer, see if you can spot people who are doing things wrong when they cross the road, like talking on their mobile phone or running instead of walking.

Walking buses

Hundreds of primary schools around England now have their own 'walking bus' scheme. On a 'walking bus' children walk together in a group, with adult leaders to escort them to school along an agreed route. It's often parent volunteers who lead the bus. Children can join the 'bus' along the route. It's a way of getting to school that is safe and sociable and doesn't add to traffic congestion and pollution.

Sounds like a good idea? Many local authorities will help schools that want to set up walking buses. Contact the school travel adviser at your local authority, who should be able to tell you more and even help you get a walking bus started at your child's school.

The Department of Transport is even offering cash to get walking buses set up – primary schools can apply for a grant to set up a new walking bus or to promote walking to school.

See www.walkingbus.com and www.dft.gov.uk for information on funding.

Count your steps – pedometers for schools

The government has launched a National School Pedometer Programme to tackle childhood obesity. The idea is that giving kids pedometers will encourage them to be active.

Two hundred and fifty schools in specially chosen areas will get a total of 45,000 pedometers under the scheme, launched in January 2007.

A successful pilot scheme in fifty schools showed that using a pedometer does increase children's activity levels – and it works particularly well with less active pupils. It also had a knock-on effect with families, as children persuaded the parents to go for country walks at the weekend to increase their totals.

If you think your child's school might be interested in applying for the pedometer scheme, there's information at the Youth Sport Trust's website www.schoolsonthemove.co.uk about which schools are eligible.

If your children don't get a pedometer through school, you could buy one for them. Better still, buy one for yourself too, and try my challenge opposite!

Kelly's family challenge

- Using your pedometers, keep a record of the total number of steps you do in a week. At the end of the week, give a prize to the person who has done the most steps.

- The following week, give a prize to the person who has increased their total by the biggest amount!.

Make a star chart!

We all love to be praised.

"Well done!"

"That was great"

"You are a star!"

Praise like this encourages the child to do the same thing again. So you can use praise to reward children when they have done something good. You can also use rewards in a more systematic way to motivate your child, using a star chart or reward programme.

For instance, suppose you would like your child to walk to school with a friend, but at the moment they always take so long to get ready for school that there isn't time to walk and you end up having to drive them there in the car. You could try a reward chart system.

How does it work?
Every time your child successfully achieves the 'target' behaviour, they get a star or sticker on the chart. For young children, the stickers and your praise and attention alone may be enough to motivate them.

With older children, you may need to set up a system so that your child earns a reward when they have a certain number of stickers or stars. (In the interests of a healthy diet, though, don't let them choose junk food or sweets as a reward too often!)

How to set up your programme
- Be clear about what you want them to do, e.g. 'Leave on time and walk to school'.
- Involve them in planning the reward programme.
- If you are going to offer rewards, work out with them what these could be.
- Stars and stickers can earn them a reward – this makes every star a small reward in itself.
- Don't expect too much all at once. Set goals they can achieve.
- If they can exchange stickers for rewards, plan it so they don't have to earn too many for a reward, or they may lose patience.
- Don't remove stars or rewards as a punishment – once they've earned them, they should keep them.
- If they don't manage it, try to be positive.
- Be flexible – you may need to adjust the goals or the rewards as time goes on.
- Once they have got into the habit of walking to school, you may want to phase out the tangible rewards.
- Remember to keep encouraging and praising them.
- Children usually respond to reward programmes for three or four weeks.

MY STAR CHART!

my goal: to leave on time and walk to school

week 1	stars I have earned							
Monday	★	★	★	★	★	★	★	☆
Tuesday	★	★	★	★	★	★	★	☆
wednesday	★	★	★	★	★	★	★	☆
Thursday	★	★	★	★	★	★	★	☆
Friday	★	★	★	★	★	★	★	☆
week 2								
Monday	★	★	★	★	★	★	★	☆
Tuesday	★	★	★	★	★	★	★	☆
wednesday	★	★	★	★	★	★	★	☆
Thursday	★	★	★	★	★	★	★	☆
Friday	★	★	★	★	★	★	★	☆
week 3								
Monday	★	★	★	★	★	★	★	☆
Tuesday	★	★	★	★	★	★	★	☆
wednesday	★	★	★	★	★	★	★	☆
Thursday	★	★	★	★	★	★	★	☆
Friday	★	★	★	★	★	★	★	☆

Cycle to school

I grew up in a village in Kent – Hildenborough – and went to secondary school in Tonbridge. There was no bus to Tonbridge, so I used to cycle three miles there and three miles back. From the age of twelve I did it on my own but by the time I was fourteen some boys from the village were also going there.

I used to set up challenges with the local boys – I was always very competitive. I would speed off ahead and beat them to school!

Cycling is good news for kids!

Cycling is much faster than walking but uses the same amount of energy.

Cycling keeps you fit. And because bikes are pedal-powered they don't pollute the planet with fumes.

Bikeability

Do you remember doing your 'cycling proficiency' test at school when you were a kid?

From spring 2007 there will be a new cycling training scheme, Bikeability, which is being called 'cycling proficiency for the 21st century'.

It aims to give kids the skills and confidence they need to cycle safely on today's roads. The idea is also to make cycling more of an everyday activity – because it's a good way for kids to get exercise.

Bikeability has three different levels
- Level 1 is where you learn to control your bike.
- Level 2 is where you start with real traffic, but sticking to quiet roads.
- Level 3 is where you can move up to busy roads and advanced road features. It's like driving or motorbike lessons and once you have done it you should be able to bike most places safely, certainly after some practice. Normally you will do this once you have started secondary school.

The Bikeability trainers will give you clear advice on what trips your child is trained to make. Then it will be up to you to encourage them to practise as much as possible, so they will remember what they have learned and build up experience.

The aim is that within five years, no child should leave primary school without the opportunity to have Bikeability training.

For more information, see www.bikeability.org.uk.

Making playgrounds more fun

For too long many school playgrounds have been concrete, featureless places that don't encourage children to play or be active.

I'm happy to say that now more and more schools are transforming their playgrounds in various ways – landscaping, adding interesting features and even training school dinner ladies and older children to lead games.

Changing playground culture

I'm proud to be associated with the Youth Sport Trust and one of their projects, in partnership with Nike and the Department for Education and Skills, is to improve playgrounds. Called Zoneparc/Sporting Playgrounds, the idea is that school playgrounds are redesigned in a way that increases children's and young people's activity levels.

Also, lunchtime supervisors and some older pupils get training so they can be playground leaders and help organise activities in the playground.

Since it started in 2001, over 330 schools are using the Zoneparc concept in their playgrounds.

The playground is re-designed into three colour-coded zones:

- **The red zone is a court area for traditional sports like rugby, football, tennis, cricket, netball and basketball**
- **The blue zone is for activities like skipping and using equipment for balancing and target games**
- The yellow zone is the chill-out zone, for chatting and quiet play such as board games – it has seating in the shade
- The 'heart line' is an orange line that runs around the playground linking all three zones together – kids can run round it for fun and fitness

The great thing about this scheme is that it changes the culture of the playground. It solves a lot of playground problems, because kids are too busy enjoying themselves with the equipment, activities and games to get into arguments.

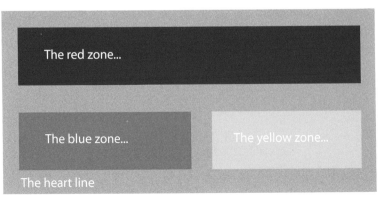

The red zone...

The blue zone...

The yellow zone...

The heart line

An example of a zoned playground

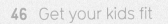

The results show:

- Children are more active
- They use their imagination more to make up games
- Their skills increase
- The use of the playground space is much fairer – it's not dominated by any one group
- Girls have more opportunities to take part in playground activities
- There is less bullying and fighting
- There is a 'sanctuary' for those who want to get away from the hurly-burly
- Fewer playtime injuries result
- Lunchtime supervisors are more motivated
- Noncompetitive children are not left out

'You rarely see a child standing around doing nothing. I love to see a game involving children from Year 1 up to Year 6, and this happens regularly.'

Classroom assistant, Enfield

Does your child's playground need a makeover?

Does the playground at your child's school needs some improvement? If so, why not ask the head teacher if he or she would like you to lead a group of parents in taking on this project? Willing and enthusiastic volunteers with good organisational skills are a godsend to busy school heads.

Here are some of the really important parts of the initiative that no playground should be without for more information see www.youthsporttrust.org/page/zone-parc.

Zone the playground

- To stop certain activities dominating the whole playground, zone different areas for sports, free play and quiet play
- Brightly coloured areas make the zones clear and often inspire children to be more active
- Make sure the children understand the zones and markings
- Allocate play leaders to each area

Offer a range of activities

- Offer three to five different activities in each zone
- Offer activities that encourage children to play together, such as relay games
- Think about new activities, such as circus skills and cheerleading, that may appeal to kids who don't like traditional sports
- What about a dance or theatre area, with music?

Provide enough equipment

- Have bright, safe, durable equipment for activities
- Have enough for all the children to be active
- Set up a fair system for borrowing or returning playground equipment
- Think about where equipment could be stored safely and securely

Organise training for playground leaders

- Your local education authority might offer playground training to teachers, lunchtime supervisors and classroom assistants
- Play leaders could work towards qualifications in play management or sports leadership
- Parents with the relevant skills/training could also run sports and activities

Allow children to take on responsibility

- Older children could be trained as play leaders with responsibility for organising activities, guiding younger children and distributing and collecting equipment
- Recruit them through nomination and election, or application and interview
- Give play leaders special bibs or bands to identify them in the playground
- Consider approaching your local secondary school to see if they have any pupils who wish to volunteer as 'junior sports leaders'

Provide challenges and competitions

- Set challenges for children that promote co-operation, problem-solving and teamwork
- Set targets for physical activity
- Reward commitment and participation in activities
- Consider competitions to keep pupils interested – such as designing and introducing a game to the other children

Use of rotas

- Think about organising a rota to offer children a variety of activities
- Rotating the roles of play leaders helps them learn different skills and keeps them interested – e.g. distributing and collecting equipment on one day, leading a new activity on another day

Making schools healthier

Schools can play a role in preventing obesity in their pupils.

In the 'National Healthy Schools Programme', schools are awarded 'Healthy School Status' if they are doing good work on:

- Physical activity
- Healthy eating
- Personal, social and health education
- Emotional health and wellbeing

They have to show they are trying to tackle obesity with:

- The meals and food they provide in school
- What they teach pupils about food
- The provision of plenty of PE and sports in and outside school hours

Schools should also work with parents and carers to:

- Provide opportunities for them to get involved in physical activities – such as helping to run after-school clubs and sports days
- Help them understand the benefits of physical activity

Some schools are also arranging activities for pupils and their families to do together, such as vegetable-growing clubs and cooking clubs.

Investing in young people

Schools are very keen to use their talented young people and this is being reflected in the amount of leadership training children are given. Even children in primary school are being given leadership responsibilities.

Luttonden Dene school in Kirklees asks its eleven-year-olds to apply to become playground leaders. After the application they are interviewed and, if successful, issued with a special sweatshirt and then given training to help younger children in the playground.

And Sports Leaders UK now have a special Young Leader Award for children aged nine to thirteen.

This kind of leadership initiative is reflected throughout schools and in secondary school children get the chance to:

- ● Lead activities in PE lessons
- ● Help with after-school clubs
- ● Run festivals for primary schools with the Youth Sport Trust TOP link scheme
- ● Take awards designed by Sports Leaders UK
- ● Attend leadership camps run by County Sport Partnerships
- ● Work as leaders overseas

Chapter 4
What goes on inside schools?

I believe that it is really important that you are aware of what your child is being taught at school so you can help to develop their skills at home. You might think, What's the point of PE lessons? But you'd be surprised at the many positive effects that taking part in sports at school can have on your kids, from boosting their confidence to even helping them concentrate in their maths lessons!

I think that parents often don't know enough about what their children are doing in PE at school and what they are learning about health and fitness. The national curriculum can sometimes seem a bit of a mystery, but this chapter explains what your kids are learning – and should be expected to do – at different stages in their education.

PE – what's it good for?

Sport and fitness have so many benefits beyond simply keeping your kids healthy. They give children confidence in their own ability to achieve and boost their self-esteem. It can help them make friends and it helps their communication skills both with other kids their age and with adults.

If your children do competitive sport – at any level and at any age – they will learn how to deal with failure and how to keep going.

Children can achieve something really positive through sport. When you are releasing energy out on the playing field, you get a real adrenalin rush. Time flies when you are doing something you enjoy.

I just loved to give everything a go – I loved being outdoors and learning. And once I was achieving something, that feeling of success really spurred me on. It wasn't even winning that mattered, it was just that I was getting better. Then I found athletics, at the age of twelve.

You don't know what your child's talent is until they get the chance to try different activities. And you don't see them at school, so you don't necessarily find out what they are good at. So parents need to know more about what happens in school and what their child enjoys and is good at, so they can build on it.

Sport can help them learn

Many schools acknowledge that PE can actually help children learn. Specialist Sports Colleges are leading the way by showing how a focus on learning through PE can help the whole school gain much better GCSE results. But there are many reason why doing sports and PE can help your kids do better in the classroom:

- Co-ordination learned through handling and throwing objects in PE helps the hand movements required in writing
- Early-morning 'Brain Gym' and yoga-type activities help children pay attention for longer
- Children are less disruptive after taking part in well-organised activities at lunchtime
- Success in PE leads to greater self-esteem
- Some schools find the teaching of languages is easier if done through PE
- Children enjoy the responsibility of being a captain, blowing a whistle, keeping time, taking part of the PE lesson, and such activities help them see the point of making a contribution to school and community life

Physical education develops children's physical competence and confidence

PE provides opportunities for kids to be creative, competitive and to face up to different challenges as individuals and in groups and teams. It promotes positive attitudes towards active and healthy lifestyles.

Children discover their aptitudes, abilities and preferences, and make choices about how to get involved in lifelong physical activity.

This is what high-quality PE and sport in school can give to children and young people:

- Commitment
- Understanding
- Healthy active lifestyle
- Confidence
- Skills
- Participation in different types of activities
- Thinking and decision-making
- Desire to improve
- Stamina, suppleness and strength
- Enjoyment

The school should keep you well informed about your child's experiences, progress and achievement. The government wants all schools to provide at least two hours of physical activity for pupils each week, including both lessons and extracurricular activities like after-school clubs.

(in normal language!)

The National Curriculum sets out what the government says children should be learning at different ages in every school subject. It says what schools should cover and sets targets for children's learning or performance; it's then up to individual schools and teachers to decide how to teach it.

Schools are also expected to make sure all pupils have the chance to succeed, whatever their individual needs and abilities.

What the National Curriculum says...	...and what it means!
Acquiring and developing skills	Learning things like throwing, catching and dribbling a ball or performing a particular dance movement.
Selecting and applying skills, tactics and 'compositional ideas'	For instance, planning approaches to their performance in a gym or dance routine, or tactics in a football, rugby or netball match.
Evaluating and improving performance	Children need to be able to try things out, solve problems, make mistakes and work out how well they are doing and how to do better.
Knowledge and understanding of fitness and health	Children identify and investigate things like stamina, suppleness, strength and speed and how they affect their bodies. They need to learn about safe and effective exercising and training.

The main things your children learn during Key Stage 1

This is what your child should be expected to do during Key Stage 1, ages five to seven. You can help them develop these skills at home by trying some of the activities that follow.

Area of activity	Your kids will learn to...
Dance activities	Use movement imaginatively; change rhythm, speed, level and direction; create and perform simple dances; express and communicate ideas and feelings
Games	Travel with, send and receive a ball in different ways; take part in simple net games, striking/fielding games (e.g. rounders, cricket) and invasion-type games (like rugby); play simple competitive games
Gymnastics	Perform basic skills on floor and using apparatus; develop the range of skills (e.g. balancing, taking off and landing, turning and rolling); create and perform short sequences, changing direction, level and speed
Swimming (schools don't have to teach swimming, but many do)	Move in water; float and move with and without swimming aids; propel themselves in water using different swimming aids, arm and leg actions and basic strokes

Encourage your child to learn basic skills

Not every child is going to enjoy every sport, or be good at it. Different kids enjoy different things. What really matters is that they are physically active.

The key things kids need to develop first are agility, balance and co-ordination. You need these for any activity – if you are running, for example, but also if you are catching or throwing a ball.

At a young age, children need to learn good movement skills and understand how to control their bodies.

Movement skills such as running, jumping and turning form the basis of most sports, and between the ages of seven and twelve, children are ready to acquire these skills.

They need to develop a movement 'vocabulary' – agility, balance, co-ordination, running, jumping, throwing, catching, twisting, turning, hand-eye co-ordination, rhythm and power – before they choose to specialise in specific sports.

But even before this, they need to do PE – it creates a solid base from which they can go on to develop these fundamental skills.

Help develop your child's balance

- Get your child to balance on their right leg for a count of five
- Can they do the same on their left leg?
- When they can do this, get them to balance on their toes for a count of five, standing on their right leg
- Can they do the same on the left leg?
- Can they balance for a count of ten?
- Can they balance while walking along a line on the floor?
- Make it harder by getting them to balance along something like a low wall
- As they improve, challenge them by finding higher and thinner places for them to test their balance!

Kelly's challenge:

Teach your child to throw and catch

- Get your child to throw a light ball up in the air and catch it

- When they can do this, move on to throwing it back and forwards between you

- When they can do this, move further apart

- Then move even further apart!

- Switch to a smaller ball and go through the same stages again

- When children are successfully throwing and catching the ball, try making things harder by making up challenges.

Improve your child's skills

Many primary schools use TOP Play, a programme of activities designed for children aged four to nine years. It starts with basic skills for the youngest children and progresses to more challenging activities for the older ones. It was designed by the Youth Sport Trust.

Try these activities and simple teaching tips to help children get better.

Short sprint

Try asking your child to run quickly in the garden, in a park or when in a safe space. Choose an obvious target to run towards. They'll love it even more if you run too. When running encourage children to:

- Run on the balls of their feet
- Swing their arms in the direction of the run
- Lean the body slightly forwards
- Stop with control by putting the weight on the front foot and bringing the other foot alongside
- Practise dodging and swerving as well

Rolling

Rolling a ball is a great activity for encouraging co-ordination and aiming. You can roll towards a target to knock it down (plastic cups, skittles). This is a great motivator as everyone wants to carry on until everything is knocked over. You can also roll to someone else or even make a small golf course where children roll or throw towards several 'holes', seeing how few rolls or throws they can take.

When rolling encourage children to:

- Get low to the ground
- Have the opposite foot to the rolling arm forward
- Hold the ball in their fingers or palm
- Follow through towards the target when they release the ball

Throwing

All children want to throw. It's best to have a wall and target or encourage throwing down into the floor to encourage children to throw hard. For accuracy you can also use a target or throw to someone else. You could also play a game of 'throw squash' against a wall.

When throwing encourage children to:
- Hold the ball in their fingers (rather than their palm)
- When throwing overarm, hold the other arm up for balance and aim
- Have the opposite foot forward when throwing
- Look towards the target
- Follow through towards the target when they release the ball

Kicking

Kicking practices are similar to the ones for throwing. They are best done against a wall with a target. If playing with a goalkeeper make sure everyone gets a fair turn.

When kicking encourage children to:
- Kick the ball for accuracy and short distances with the side of the foot
- Kick the ball with the top of the foot (laces) when kicking for distance or power
- Place the non-kicking foot down alongside the ball
- Watch the ball at all times
- Keep their head over the ball when they kick it

Batting

There are lots of simple batting games. The key thing is to make sure children can hit the ball, so make it big enough, bowl it slowly enough and make it bounce as many times as it takes for children to be successful. It's best to start off with a small bat.

When striking a ball encourage children to:

- Stand sideways
- Use a short 'backlift'
- Hold the bat or racquet with a firm grip as though they were shaking hands

Catching

Catching or receiving a ball tends to get less practice than throwing or kicking, but it is very important. Ensure when you play games to practise receiving that they are always co-operative. How many times can we catch the ball together? How many times can we pass to each other? Can we pass this ball around the circle before the person has run round it?

When catching encourage children to:
- Make a target with their hands to help the person throwing
- Cup their hands to receive the ball
- Watch the flight of the ball
- Cushion the ball into their hands

The school sports scene: the lowdown for parents

The National School Sport Strategy

The government has set a target to increase the amount of sport that children and young people are doing. Its School Sport Strategy sets out ways to reach this target:

1 Sports Colleges

Secondary schools can apply for 'specialist status' and become a specialist Sports College, focusing on raising pupils' achievment in PE and sport.

2 School Sport Partnerships

Chances are your child's school is part of one of these already – all state schools in England belong to one of 450 School Sport Partnerships. The idea is that 'families' of schools work together to improve sports opportunities for all their pupils.

3 More training for teachers

There is training for PE teachers and others to improve the quality of their teaching. The training will also encourage teachers to be more innovative so they can provide activities that will meet the needs of all pupils, not just the sporty ones.

4 Step into Sport

Step into Sport gets young people aged fourteen to nineteen involved in leadership and volunteering through sport.

They can experience sports leadership, gain leadership qualifications, help children in primary schools organise festivals of sport, and take up local sports volunteering placements.

5 Gifted and talented kids

We need to identify and support kids who are particularly good at PE and school sport so they don't slip through the net. So a network of multi-skill academies is being set up to help talented young athletes fulfil their potential.

6 Sporting playgrounds

Children spend around 25 per cent of the school day in the playground. Traditionally playgrounds are often dull, uninspiring and intimidating for many children. Often, just a few children dominate the whole area. So improving playtimes can have a big impact on school life.

More and more schools are introducing the Zoneparc model to increase physical activity levels and improve behaviour in the playground. You can read all about this – and how to introduce it in your own child's school – on page 46.

7 Swimming

Advice is being given to schools on how to encourage more children to take up and enjoy swimming. All schools have to teach swimming and water safety in Key Stage 2 as part of the National Curriculum (see page 70).

Schools have changed. But as parents you need to be aware of what your children are being offered – and voice your concern if you don't think they are getting enough PE and sport

Competition in schools – a good thing?

In past decades, some schools have had a slightly negative attitude towards competitive sports. There was an idea that competition was somehow not fair to less able children. But that sometimes meant that talented young people who were good at sport missed out on the chance to excel.

I'm pleased to say that this is changing. There's been a shake-up in the way competitive sport is organised in schools and beyond, and children today stand to benefit from these changes. This is true whatever their ability level, because competing doesn't only benefit the children who are particularly good at sport. I believe it helps to motivate kids at every level and extends their skills.

At my primary school, although my racing achievements were limited to winning the egg-and-spoon and the sack races on school sports day, I was prefect and games captain for my house. I was good at all the games so everyone always wanted to be on my team. Because I had the pick of the best, we nearly always won!

Schools now **must** provide competitive games activities throughout Key Stages 1 to 3 (ages five to fourteen).

After that, at Key Stage 4, pupils can choose other activities instead of competitive team and individual games. But schools are still expected to provide these for pupils who want them.

Competition motivates children – who doesn't enjoy scoring points and winning? Competition does not always have to be at a high level but those kids who love to try and be the best should be given the chance to compete and excel.

There's now a framework for competitive sport in schools, which goes like this:

- Multi-skills festivals with the emphasis on fun in Key Stages 1 and 2
- Multi-sports competitions in Key Stages 2 and 3
- Access to inter-school leagues and competitions by Key Stages 3 and 4
- For talented young sportspeople, this can lead to the UK School Games
- This can link up with what young people do in sports and athletics clubs outside school. They can progress from playing at junior level to men's or ladies' teams, then at county level, then at regional level. Those who make it to playing at national level could even get spotted by the England selectors and go all the way to the Olympics!

But – to get back to schools – all schools have a wide range of sporting ability among their students.

Across the country, 'competition managers' will link with local sporting networks to help set up competitions, events and leagues between schools. They will also integrate school sport with sports clubs in the community. That way, talented young people can progress from the simplest school competitions right through to the Olympics if they are good enough.

The competition managers make sure competitions are not just for the most sporty children. There are different levels of competition, allowing less able or less experienced children to take part in competitive sports too. As well as the A team, you might have a B, C and D team or a novices' team, for instance.

Competition isn't just about elite athletes and gold medals. Anyone can learn vital skills by competing. It teaches valuable life skills.

In some activities, children can also 'compete' against themselves, trying to beat their own previous performance.

The main things your children learn in Key Stage 2

During Key Stage 2 (from age seven to eleven) children enjoy being active and using their creativity and imagination. They learn new skills, use them in different ways and link them to make sequences. They enjoy communicating, collaborating and competing with each other.

During this Key Stage, pupils should be taught through five types of activity: dance, games and gymnastics are compulsory, plus two from swimming and water safety, athletics activities, and outdoor and adventurous activities. The school has to offer swimming unless pupils have already done it during Key Stage 1.

Area of activity	Your kids will learn to...
Dance activities	Create and perform dances using a range of movements; respond to a range of stimuli and accompaniment (e.g. music, drumbeats)
Games activities	Play and make up small-sided competitive net, striking/fielding and invasion games; use skills and tactics and apply basic principles for attacking and defending; work with others to organise and keep the games going
Gymnastic activities	Create and perform sequences on the floor and using apparatus; vary the level, speed and direction in their sequences
Swimming activities and water safety	Pace themselves in floating and swimming challenges related to speed, distance and personal survival; swim unaided for at least 25 metres; use recognised arm and leg actions, on their front and back; use a range of strokes and personal survival skills
Athletic activities	Take part in and design challenges and competitions that call for precision, speed, power or stamina; use running, jumping and throwing skills – on their own and in combination; pace themselves in these challenges and competitions
Outdoor and adventurous activities	Take part in outdoor activity challenges, including following trails in familiar and unfamiliar environments; use a range of orienteering and problem-solving skills; work with others to meet the challenges

What happens next – The National Curriculum in secondary schools

In Key Stage 3 (age eleven to fourteen) your kids will become more expert in their skills and techniques and learn to apply them in different activities. At the moment the curriculum is under review and changes are due to take place from September 2008.

The key objectives of these changes are to help all young people to:

- **Develop skills in physical activity**
- **Be creative and make decisions**
- **Develop physical and mental capacity**
- **Evaluate and improve their own and others' performance**
- **Make informed choices about healthy, active lifestyles**
- **Take on different roles and responsibilities such as coach, official or leader**

These objectives will be achieved through a challenging, inspiring and flexible curriculum which will enable all young people achieve

Choosing the right trainers

Kids do need trainers for school sport, because shoes and plimsolls don't give enough support. But cheap trainers are as effective as the expensive ones, as long as:

- **They have cushioning (the white part of the trainer above the sole) to limit the impact on the joints when the child is running or jumping**
- **They fit correctly, to avoid blisters**
- **They are not too tight over the top of the foot**
- **They are not too big, as this lessens the support around the foot**

You don't need any gimmicks. And brand names are not an issue for me. I know that children always want the 'in' thing and it can be expensive for parents – but if you can't or don't want to pay high prices, a cheap pair can be just as good.

Sporting champions who inspired me

Watching sports stars can be inspiring for children and young people. I remember watching Sebastian Coe win the 1500 metres at the Los Angeles Olympics in 1984, when I was fourteen. He was absolutely elated. What an inspiration. I wondered what it would feel like to be so good at your sport that you could qualify to perform in the Olympics . . .

When I was a teenager, my other sporting inspiration – but for different reasons – was Tessa Sanderson, who had won an Olympic gold for the javelin in 1984. Our family were at a Butlin's holiday camp in Skegness and she turned up to take some of the fitness competitions. I won all the competitions that I entered and so proudly had my photograph taken with her. But in fact what impressed me most was her car. It was plush, streamlined and silver with a javelin painted down its side. I remember thinking, 'Oh my God, I'd love to have that!'

Helping in school

Your time and enthusiasm can make a difference. Many parents volunteer to help in school with PE and sport alongside the PE teachers. This makes it easier for schools to deliver high-quality sport, because there is often a shortage of adults to help.

Particularly when teachers take pupils off the school site, they often need to have one or two extra adults with them.

If you are experienced in a particular sport, you can be a great role model. But even if you're not, your involvement could really improve pupils' experience of PE and sport.

How you can help

- Lead playground activities in primary school
- Help the PE teacher in PE lessons and school sport
- Support the school teams as a coach, referee or other official
- Help out with after-school sports clubs
- Help with one-off events like sports days

What you choose to do depends on the opportunities available at the school, your interests and how much time you can spare.

If you can't help on a regular weekly basis, perhaps you could offer a day or a few days to help with sports days, sports festivals or team matches.

Chapter 5
Eat well, stay healthy

I believe that healthy eating is all about balance. It's not about banning certain foods or giving things up altogether – it's all about finding that healthy balance so that all the nutritional needs are met.

Schools are currently having a big push on healthy eating, which is fantastic news. Eating a healthy diet is important for children's health, their weight, their mood and behaviour, even their ability to concentrate.

Healthy habits

We need to make sure that our kids don't develop bad habits like overeating, missing breakfast and living on junk food.

You can't force children and young people to do anything, so I believe the best approach is to help them to make the right choices for themselves.

You can help them see how the quality of the food they eat affects their health and weight, and help them understand what makes for a balanced diet. You can encourage them to take an interest in what they eat, such as food quality and where our food comes from.

Teaching them to cook is a great idea too!

What to tell your children about food

There are five different food groups:

- Bread, cereals, rice, potatoes
- Vegetables and fruit
- Meat, poultry, fish, eggs, nuts, beans and pulses
- Milk, yogurt and cheese
- Food containing fats and oils, and foods and drinks containing sugar

The food pyramid

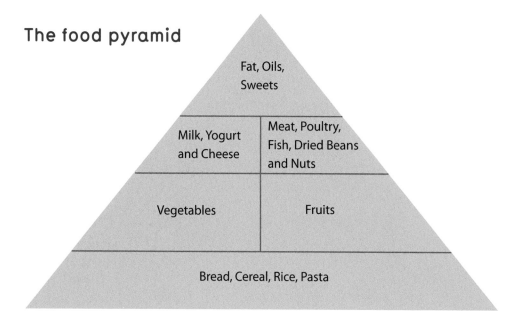

We should eat a variety of foods from the first five groups, at the bottom of the pyramid, on a regular basis. The higher up the pyramid, the less of that food we need. We should eat only small amounts of foods containing fat and sugar.

Bread, cereals, rice and potatoes provide growing children with energy and kids can eat lots of food from this group. These are starchy foods or CARBOHYDRATES. Starchy food should make up a third of what we eat every day.

Vegetables and fruit provide VITAMINS, MINERALS and FIBRE, which help protect us from illness.

Meat, poultry, fish, eggs, beans, lentils and nuts are all sources of PROTEIN. Protein repairs and renews cells and muscles, and children need protein to grow.

Milk, cheese and yogurt (dairy products) provide calcium, which strengthens bones and teeth and also helps our nerves and muscles to work. Non-dairy sources of calcium include: almonds, brazil nuts, bread, chickpeas, dried fruit and sardines.

Fats should only be eaten in small amounts. Children need some fat, which will provide them with energy and body warmth, but we should steer clear of certain fat types (see pages 79).

Don't eat more calories than you are burning up

The amount of energy that food gives us is measured in calories (kcal). If you are active and do a lot of walking, running, playing outside or sport, you burn more calories. If you sit down all day, you burn fewer calories.

But if you take in more calories than you burn – in other words, if you eat more than you need – your body will store what's left over as fat.

Different people have different energy (calorie) needs, depending on their sex and age and how active they are. Children need a lot more energy and nutrients for their body size than adults do.

How many calories do your kids need?

These are the estimated guideline daily amounts for boys and girls

	Boys	Girls
7–10 years	1,970	1,740
11–14 years	2,200	1,845
15–18 years	2,755	2,110

Five a Day

There can't be many people who don't know by now that we should eat at least five helpings of fruit and vegetables a day. But many kids still don't manage this.

Kelly's five-a-day challenge

Help your kids reach their target:

- Help them spot all the vegetables they are eating, such as vegetables 'hidden' in casseroles and curries.
- Put peas and chopped or grated carrot in shepherd's pie or pieces of courgette in lasagne. Add slices of pepper and other veg to pizza toppings. Mix in some mashed carrot, parsnip or swede if you are making mashed potato.
- Try making your own milkshakes and smoothies by blending puréed fruit with milk or yogurt.

What can you count in your five-a-day?

- Vegetables – raw, cooked on their own or in other dishes, frozen or canned
- Salad
- Fruit – fresh, frozen, stewed or canned – or fruit juice
- Dried fruit

What doesn't count?

- Potatoes
- Fruit juice and smoothies can only count as one portion a day, however much you drink!

Sugar

We all know that kids love sugar. Sugar energy is immediate – but it soon fades, and then you want another drink or more food. And sugar doesn't provide our bodies with any nutrients, or anything else but energy (calories) – that's why it's sometimes called 'empty calories'.

If kids are hungry, it's better to fill up on starchy food like bread, which is a healthier source of calories than fat or sugar.

Cutting down on sugar

When buying food, watch out on the ingredients list for other words used to describe sugar, such as sucrose, glucose (syrup), fructose, hydrolysed starch and invert sugar. The higher up the ingredients list they come, the higher in sugar the foods are.

Salt – what's so bad about it?

Salt contains sodium and having too much sodium can cause high blood pressure. And people with high blood pressure are three times more likely to develop heart disease or have a stroke than people with normal blood pressure.

Most of us, including children, eat too much salt. But the problem is not necessarily that we add salt to our food – it is our over-reliance on processed foods, which have a high salt content compared with most natural, unprocessed food.

If children have too much salt, it could affect their health in the future. And it could also give them a taste for salty food so that they carry on eating too much salt as adults. The maximum amount of salt a child should have depends on their age:

- **4–6 years – 3g a day (1.2g sodium)**
- **7–10 years – 5g a day (2g sodium)**
- **11 and over (that means adults too) – 6g a day (2.5g sodium)**

Because kids should have less salt than adults, a ready-meal or other food that's high in salt will take them even closer to their daily recommended maximum than it would for an adult.

See www.salt.gov.uk/salt_calculator.shtml for an easy way to calculate what percentage of the daily salt limit your child is having.

Fats in food

We all need a small amount of fat in our diet to keep healthy. But there are different types of fat, and some are much better for us than others.

Saturated fat can raise blood cholesterol, which clogs up our arteries and causes heart disease. Saturated fats are usually solid at room temperature and come mostly from animal sources, such as butter, lard and suet.

Hydrogenated trans fats are produced in food manufacturing processes to solidify the cheapest vegetable oils. These fats are used in takeaways, ready-meals, cakes, biscuits, crisps and sauces. Like saturated fats, they raise the risk of heart disease.

Kelly's Healthy Alternatives!

To cut down on saturated fat:

- **Choose low-fat alternatives to butter, margarine, mayonnaise or salad dressings**
- **Use full-fat cheese or cheese spreads sparingly**
- **Watch out for meat pies, pasties, fried foods and salami, because these tend to be high in fat**
- **Choose lean cuts of meat and take the skin off chicken**

Unsaturated fats are normally soft or liquid at room temperature and are usually vegetable fats. Good sources include oily fish, nuts and seeds, avocado, sunflower and olive oil.

Essential fatty acids. You've probably heard of omega-3 and omega-6. We don't need much of the omega-6 fatty acids (found in most vegetable oils), and we need them in the right balance: we should have more omega-3 than 6. Omega-3 fatty acids are the healthiest of all fats and are found in oily fish and some vegetable oils, especially those made from rapeseed, walnut and flaxseeds. They help protect against heart disease and cancer.

Fish food

We should all try to eat at least two servings of fish a week, including one serving of oily fish. Oily fish, such as salmon, sardines and mackerel, contain more omega-3 than white fish. Fresh, frozen and canned fish, fish fingers and fish cakes are all good.

Fish to avoid

Children shouldn't eat shark, swordfish or marlin. This is because mercury can build up in these fish and high levels of mercury can affect a child's developing nervous system. You should avoid giving more than two portions of oily fish a week to girls, or four portions to boys. This is because pollutants can build up in the oily parts of fish. There is no need to limit the amount of other fish your children have, apart from avoiding shark, swordfish and marlin.

Fish oil: supplements or the real thing?

Some parents give their kids fish-oil tablets because they've read that it improves their concentration. But provided your kids will eat fish, it's better to give them real fish than expensive supplements because, as well as containing omega-3 fatty acids, fish is an excellent source of other nutrients.

We need water!

Water is contained in all our body tissues and makes up:
- **About 85 per cent of the brain**
- **About 80 per cent of the blood**
- **About 70 per cent of lean muscle**

We lose water from our body in a number of ways:

- As water vapour when we breathe out
- As sweat
- In urine and faeces
- Through vomiting or diarrhoea when we are ill

People can survive for six weeks without food, but only a few days if they are deprived of water. Our main source of water is in the fluids we drink, but we also get some from fresh fruits and vegetables.

Children need to drink around **six cups** of fluid each day – and water is better than sweetened drinks.

You should drink even more water than usual when you are active!

Snacks and drinks

Snacks can fill the gap between meals if you get hungry. But try to make them healthy snacks – for instance if you eat fruit or vegetables, that counts towards your 'five a day'.

Kelly's Healthy Alternatives!

- An apple or some dried fruit or carrot sticks will keep you going till you have a proper meal – but they won't spoil your appetite and they are better for you than a bag of crisps or a bar of chocolate.
- Drinking fizzy drinks or even fruit juice lots of times in a day between meals is not good for your teeth, because it means your teeth are being exposed to sugar lots of times in the day. You can drink water any time, though.
- Why not have a plate of pieces of fruit, dried fruit, nuts and carrot sticks or slices of malt bread waiting for your kids when they come in from school, starving? It's better than raiding the biscuit tin! They might say they don't want fruit – so don't ask them. Just leave it in front of them and watch them help themselves!

Yuk! I'm not eating *that*

If your child says they hate healthy food . . .

- Don't force them to eat it – simply provide healthier choices and no other options, so children learn to eat what is put in front of them
- Small taster portions for new foods are a good idea, as researchers say it takes an average of eleven 'tries' before children will accept a new food

Breakfast – the best way to start the day

Evidence shows that kids who don't eat breakfast tend to gain weight. If they feel hungry by break time, chances are they end up snacking on something sugary or high in fat. So send your kids off to school with a bowl of wholewheat cereal or some toast inside them. It gives them energy to cope with a busy morning at school, helps them concentrate and will keep them going till lunchtime. As kids get older, they often skip breakfast because they are in a rush in the mornings. So set the alarm for fifteen minutes earlier!

Read the label

Foods like ready-meals and pre-packed sandwiches can contain surprisingly different levels of fat, sugar and salt. Front-of-pack labelling should now give clear information on fat, sugar and salt so we can make healthier choices about what we buy.

Use the guide below from the Food Commission to judge whether it's nice and nutritious – or just junk.

Amount per 100g (or per serving if larger than 100g)		
	This is a lot	This is a little
Total fat	20g	3g
Saturated fat	5g	1g
Sugar	10g	2g
Sodium (salt)	0.5g (1.25g)	0.1g (0.25g)

Guideline Daily Amounts

This tells you the **maximum** you should be having, per day, of the following. (It's not a target!)

	Sugar	Fat	Saturates
Adults	90g	70g	20g
Children aged 5–10	85g	70g	20g

Ideally, we should choose foods that keep us within these limits, and we do this by reading the labels.

Try to choose foods low in fat, sugar and salt so you don't go over the limits above. No one wants to be doing maths at every meal, of course. But it's an interesting exercise to add it up on a couple of days to find out how you and your kids are doing.

The School Food Revolution

Thanks to campaigning by the Children's Food Campaign, Jamie Oliver and others, the Department for Education brought in new rules in 2006 to improve food in schools.

The new rules for food in school are:

- **No** fizzy drinks or chocolate or crisps to be sold in vending machines or tuck shops
- **Restricted** – manufactured meat products
- **Restricted** – deep-fried foods (no item served more than twice in the week)

More of the good stuff

- High-quality meat, poultry or oily fish served regularly
- A minimum of two portions of fruit and vegetables served with every meal
- Schools and vending providers should promote healthy snacks and drinks such as water, milk, fruit juices and yogurt drinks.

Active Kids Get Cooking

Active Kids Get Cooking is a fantastic initiative which promotes cooking in school, provides up-to-date information and resources for teachers about healthy eating and recognises and rewards pupils' excellent work with collectable certificates. And it's free for your child's school to register. Visit www.activekidsgetcooking.org.uk for more details.

Love that lunchbox

Trying to come up with a healthy and interesting packed lunch every day can test even the best of us – particularly when time is short. But giving your child the same thing day after day can get boring for them and doesn't provide a varied range of nutrients.

Need a bit of inspiration? Here are a few ideas for healthy packed lunches.

Making sandwiches

- Keep a selection of breads in the freezer for sandwiches. Then you can just take out what you need for one day's lunchbox and defrost it on a plate or in the microwave. If your child turns up their nose at wholemeal bread, try 'whole white' sliced bread (white bread made with one-third wholemeal flour).
- Good low-fat sandwich fillings include lean meats, fish (such as tuna or salmon), cottage cheese, Edam, mozzarella, or sliced banana.

Bored of sandwiches? Try these:

- Soup in a vacuum flask, with some wholemeal or granary bread.
- A rice salad using cooked brown rice and lentils – you could add chunks of cooked aubergine, pepper slices, chopped spring onions and pieces of cooked turkey or chicken.
- Pasta salads – mix cooked pasta with tuna and avocado, or chicken, sweet corn, cherry tomato and spinach leaves.
- A slice of pizza.
- Add some vegetables to your child's lunchbox, such as cherry tomatoes and sticks of carrot, cucumber, celery and peppers.

Kelly's Healthy Alternatives!

Healthier alternatives to sweets:

- Dried fruit, such as raisins, apricots, figs or prunes
- Stewed fruit with a spoonful or two of natural yogurt, or sprinkle some rolled oats and seeds on the top for extra crunch
- Instead of cakes, chocolates and biscuits, try scones, currant buns and fruit bread
- A slice of cheese or a yogurt provides calcium

The obesity problem

As we all know, the number of overweight and obese children is going up all the time. Obesity means someone has put on weight to the point that it could seriously endanger their health. Apart from the health risks, it's not much fun being an overweight child. You can't do the things your friends do – you can't run as fast, you feel self-conscious about your body, you can't always wear the fashions you'd like to.

What should you do if your child is overweight?

- If you are concerned about your child's weight, it's a good idea to see your doctor.
- If you think your child is eating for comfort, try and find out what is bothering them and see if you can come up with another way to tackle their worries and problems.
- If your child hates sport, try to find a physical activity they do enjoy. There are plenty to choose from in this book.
- Do more active things together as a family. It will boost your child's activity levels while they are having a good time with the people they feel most comfortable with.
- Don't keep too many cakes and biscuits in the house. It makes it too easy for them to overindulge whenever they get the urge. Have lots of fruit around instead.
- Your child doesn't need to go hungry. Wholemeal bread and pasta are good to fill up on – much better than high-fat and sugary snacks.

Eating disorders

Eating disorders include anorexia, bulimia, binge eating and compulsive overeating. Eating disorders mean someone is using food to cope with their problems – feeling bored, angry, lonely or sad – or to cope with pressure at school or in the family.

Here are some of the signs, from the self-help group the Eating Disorders Association:

Anorexia

- Severe weight loss
- Obsession with dieting
- Distorted perception of body weight and size
- Periods stopping
- Difficulty sleeping
- Dizziness
- Stomach pains
- Constipation

Bulimia

- Eating large quantities of food and being sick afterwards
- Sore throat and swollen glands
- Stomach pains
- Mouth infections

Binge-eating disorder

- Weight gain
- Eating large quantities of food
- Being secretive
- Feeling depressed and out of control
- Emotional behaviour

If you suspect your son or daughter has any of these eating disorders, you need to get help. Start by seeing your GP. For more information, see the Eating Disorders Association website on www.b-eat.co.uk.

Chapter 6

Your body

Our bodies are wonderful, amazing things. If you can instil a sense of wonder in your children about how their bodies work, then hopefully they will respect their bodies and understand that they need to keep them in good working order.

This chapter will help your child understand more about their body and why it matters that they look after it.

It's good if kids have a basic understanding of how their heart and lungs work so they can see why exercise will protect them against heart disease. And if they understand about exercise and the need for a healthy diet they are more likely to be able to maintain a healthy weight.

Your children will learn this kind of thing at school, of course, but if you want to back it up at home too, I've put together a short guide that I hope will help. You can go into more or less detail, depending on your child's age and interest.

What kids need to know about how their body works

Your heart

Your heart is a big muscle. It is about the shape of a fist. It has four chambers, or spaces, inside it.

It acts as a pump, sending blood around your body. The blood is pumped through your heart and then around your body.

Blood goes round your body in lots of narrow tubes called veins and arteries:

- **Veins take blood towards your heart**
- **Arteries take blood away from your heart**

The biggest veins and arteries go into and out of your heart. There is a network of veins and arteries, with smaller and smaller tubes like the trunk, branches and twigs of a tree. The very tiniest blood vessels are called capillaries.

Your heart is behind your ribs, on the left-hand side. Put your hand over your ribs. Can you feel your heart beating?

Run up and down the stairs three times. Try again. Can you feel it beating now? Your heart is pumping all the time.

When you move around and do exercise, you are using your muscles. Your muscles need energy to work. The blood takes energy around your body to your muscles.

So when your muscles are working harder, they need more energy from the blood. That means your heart has to work harder too – it pumps the blood faster to send more blood around your body.

That's why your heartbeat feels stronger and faster when you have been running.

Doing some activity every day is good for your heart. To stay fit, try to be active for at least an hour a day. It doesn't have to be sport – anything active, like running around in the playground, swimming and dancing, is good for you!

We have about four to five litres of blood (depending on how big we are). Look at a 1-litre squash bottle in the kitchen or supermarket – five times that amount of blood is flowing through your body!

Your lungs

When we breathe in, we take air into our lungs. Our lungs are a bit like sponges, but instead of filling with water, all the tiny spaces in them fill with air.

Around each tiny air sac in the lungs, there is a net of blood vessels. The blood collects OXYGEN from the air in our lungs.

Our body uses the oxygen and produces a waste gas called CARBON DIOXIDE. The blood brings the carbon dioxide to our lungs. When we breathe out, we get rid of the carbon dioxide.

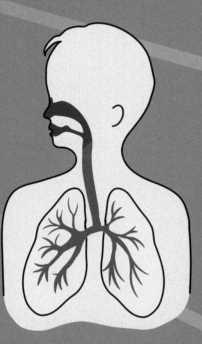

Our bodies need more oxygen when we are energetic – that's why exercise makes us breathe faster.

How do you feel when you are energetic? Puffed out? Hot?

- When we feel puffed out it's because we need to breathe faster. When we exercise, we need to take in more oxygen to make the extra energy we need to be active. Our muscles need more oxygen when they are working harder.
- We feel hot because our muscles produce heat when they are working harder.

Try this with your child:

What does exercise do to your heart rate?

- Find your pulse (you can feel a throbbing at your wrist or neck – this is the blood as it is pumped round your body)
- Choose a time when you have been sitting down for a while
- Count how many times it throbs over fifteen seconds
- Now walk round the garden or up and down the street for two minutes
- Take your pulse again and write it down
- Now jog or skip round the garden or up and down the street for two minutes
- Take your pulse again for fifteen seconds
- What has happened to it?
- Why do you think this has happened?

Your blood

Every part of your body is made of tiny bits called cells. To grow and to work properly, the cells need food and a special gas called oxygen, which comes from the air we breathe in.

Your blood flows around your body, in veins and arteries, bringing supplies of food and oxygen to all the cells of your body.

Your blood also carries nutrients from the food you eat – the body cells pick up what they need as the blood flows past them.

The blood's journey round the body

Your blood is flowing round your body all the time.

Blood flows to your lungs. In the lungs, it gets rid of waste gas (carbon dioxide) and collects oxygen. It flows round the body to the cells and muscles and gives them oxygen.

Muscles need a supply of oxygen so they can make energy to keep working. The blood then travels back to the heart, which pumps it around the body and back to the lungs so it can collect more oxygen.

Did you know?

- Blood that has oxygen in it looks red. Blood that doesn't have oxygen in it looks blue.
- Can you find a blue vein on the inside of your wrist?
- Look in the mirror and gently pull down your lower eyelid. Can you see some red thready bits? These are some of the tiniest blood vessels you have.

Your body and energy

Our bodies are using up energy all the time. We need it to grow, to keep our heart, lungs, brain, kidneys and other important organs working and to keep our body in good condition.

We get this energy from food and drink, and when we do a lot of physical activity we use up more energy.

It's important to eat the right foods and have a balance between the energy we take in and the energy our body is using up. If we keep on taking in lots of energy in food and drink that we do not use up, what do you think happens to that energy?

See page 77 for more info!

Be nice to your heart and lungs!

Don't overindulge in foods that are bad for your heart.

Foods that contain a lot of fat are bad for your heart if you eat them too often. That's because some types of fat stick to the insides of the arteries. Over a long period of time, this clogs them up. That makes it harder for blood to get round your body.

If an artery gets completely blocked, it causes a **heart attack**. This is very dangerous. People can die from heart attacks.

That's why, when you are young, you need to eat the right foods. Foods that have a lot of fat in – like crisps, chips and cakes – are foods you shouldn't have every day. Don't eat too many of them, so you will keep your heart healthy.

See page 79 to find out more!

Say no to cigarettes

Smoking is the single worst possible thing you can do for your health.

It causes heart disease. It damages your lungs. Most people who smoke had their first cigarettes when they were young teenagers. And once you start, it is very hard to stop.

Your bones and muscles

The places where your bones link up are called joints.

You have joints so you can bend your arms and legs, and your backbone has lots of joints so you can bend forwards. You have lots of little joints in your feet and ankles and they all move when you run. You have joints in your fingers and toes too.

Tough straps called **ligaments** join the bones together and hold the joints in place.

Tendons join the muscles to the bone.

Muscles allow our bodies to move.

Each joint is worked by two muscles, which work in turn. When one muscle squeezes or tightens, the other one relaxes.

Waggle your foot. Can you feel the working muscle up near your knee?

When you are a child and a teenager, your body is building 95 per cent of its bone mass. That bone mass has to last you for the rest of your life. If you take regular exercise while you are young, your bones will be stronger, so you won't be so likely to break bones when you are older. Eating foods containing **calcium** is important, too, to build healthy bones and teeth – see page 76.

What happens when exercise makes you hot and sweaty?

Your body has clever ways of cooling itself down:

Sweating

Your skin has tiny holes in the surface, called pores. Underneath are sweat glands. These are little tubes that take water and salt from your body and make sweat. When you are hot, the sweat glands make more sweat. The sweat goes out through pores on your skin. As it dries, it cools down your skin.

Going red

Your blood takes heat from your body. When you are hot, more blood moves through the vessels near the surface of your skin. (That's why your face sometimes goes red when you've been very energetic.) Then the air outside can cool it down.

Want your child to be clued up about a healthy heart?

The British Heart Foundation has some great resources to teach kids (as well as the rest of us) about the importance of looking after their hearts. Its **Artie Beat Club** is open to all 7–11-year-olds in the UK. Kids get a regular newsletter.

Schools can apply for a whole junior school membership, or you can join your child up as an individual – children always love to get post at home!

Other BHF resources include:

- *Artie Beat likes to . . .* – **an early reader for 4–5-year-olds about active play**
- *Artie Beat's picnic* – **teaching 4–6-year-olds about healthy food choices**
- *Artie Beat's body book* – **teaching 5–7-year-olds simple facts about their body**
- *Five-a-day adventure* – **a healthy-eating activity sheet with stickers of fruits and vegetables, which children can use in different ways**
- *Look after your heart* – **an activity booklet for 7–11-year-olds to explain how the heart and lungs work and how to stay healthy, with experiments to try and activity and puzzle pages (and a membership form for the Artie Beat Club on the back)**

For details on how to buy these, see the British Heart Foundation website at www.bhf.org.uk.

What children learn in school

Area of study	Key Stage 1	Key Stage 2
Personal, social and health education	How to make simple choices that affect their health and wellbeing	What makes a healthy lifestyle, including the benefits of exercise and healthy eating, what affects mental health, and how to make informed choices
Science	Taking exercise and eating the right types of food helps to keep them healthy; how skeletons and muscles support and protect bodies and help movement; importance of exercise for good health	Human life process; how the heart works; effect of exercise and rest on pulse rate
Physical Education	How important it is to be active; recognise and describe how their bodies feel during different activities	How exercise affects the body; warm up and prepare for different activities; why physical activity is good for health and wellbeing; wearing appropriate clothing and being hygienic

Differences between children and adults

Apart from the obvious differences in body size, young children and adults operate in different ways when it comes to physical activity:

- Children are much less efficient in terms of their range of movement – for instance, when they are learning to catch, they don't anticipate where the ball is going and move there.
- Their muscles are not as strong so they can't run as fast or jump as high as adults. At this age the aim of physical activity is not to build muscle.
- With children, it's more about short, sharp bursts of exercise than stamina – they can't sustain anything for very long. They perceive exercise as easier than adults so they really go for it and then just stop when they are tired.
- They have weaker bones, so any impact – such as a fall in the playground – is more likely to break a bone in a child than an adult.

When children reach puberty, they quickly start to grow in height and weight and they develop more strength and stamina.

Fancy walking round the world?

If you walked at a steady speed of 5kph (3mph) nonstop day and night, it would take you a whole year to walk round the equator – a distance of 40,000km (25,000 miles). The average person walks the equivalent of three and a half times around the earth in a lifetime.

Walk to School Campaign

Warming up

Everyone needs to understand why warming up and cooling down before and after any kind of sport or exercise is important.

Always do a warm-up before you do any sport.

You need to warm up your muscles to prevent injury problems. When you start moving around and doing some low-key aerobic exercise, this raises your heart rate and gets the blood flowing more quickly around your body. The blood takes oxygen to the muscles and ligaments, which gets them ready for the exercise you are about to do.

How warming up protects your muscles

Show your child a piece of Plasticine. Let them see how the Plasticine is likely to snap if they try to stretch it when it is cold. But if they warm it up first in their hands, it will stretch much more easily.

It's the same with muscles – warming them up increases their elasticity. If the muscle stretches more easily, your range of movement is increased. So, for instance, you will be able to move your arms and legs out further without straining your muscles.

How cooling down protects your muscles

When you have been doing intensive exercise, stopping suddenly presents too much of a shock to the body.

Gradually lowering the intensity of the exercise brings about a gradual decrease in breathing rate and heart rate. After vigorous exercise, movements of the large muscles – as in walking – help to speed up recovery by dispersing any lactic acid built up in the muscles and by assisting the veins in pumping blood back to the heart.

If your muscles have been working very hard and you don't cool down properly, you may find your muscles seize up the next day and you feel stiff.

Four steps to protect yourself from injury and stiffness:

1 Increase your pulse rate by doing some active exercise and loosening your joints

2 Once your muscles and ligaments are warmed up, do some warm-up stretches

3 Do your activity or sport

4 Cool down afterwards

1 Increase your pulse rate

Move around to get warm before you stretch your muscles. Start gently – move to music or just walk and then jog. You could run up and down the stairs or jog on the spot.

Swing your arms and legs in big circular movements. These 'loosening up' exercises prepare the joints for further activity by moving them in a controlled way to warm and circulate the synovial fluid within the joints, which allows freer, easier movement.

When you feel warm and can feel the pulse in your neck getting faster, do the stretches shown below.

2 Warm-up stretches

Do each stretch on both sides in turn. Hold each stretch for 10 seconds.

Calf stretch

Put one leg in front of the other, with your feet pointing forward. Bend your front knee. Keep your back heel down.

Side stretch

With your feet shoulder-width apart, lean to one side, reaching down towards your knee. Raise the other arm over your head. Don't bend over forwards or backwards.

Chest stretch

Clasp your hands behind your back. Lift your elbows. Keep your arms slightly bent, and keep your chest and chin up.

Back stretch

Clasp your hands in front of your body, with your arms stretched forward as though you were hugging someone. Keep your chin down. Feel the stretch across your back.

Hamstring stretch

Put one leg in front of the other, with your feet pointing forward. Bend your back knee. Straighten your front leg. Put your hands on the thigh of your bent leg.

Quadriceps stretch

Raise one foot up behind you. Hold your foot with your hand and push with your foot into your hand. Keep your knees close together. If you can't balance very well, use a wall or someone else to help you.

Back of upper arm stretch

Raise one arm above your head. Bend your arm so your hand falls behind your head. Use your free hand to push your elbow back and increase the stretch. Keep your head up and look ahead.

3 Now you are ready to play a match or do your intensive physical activity.

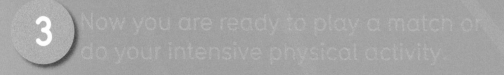

4 Cool down

After you have finished, you need to spend a few minutes bringing your pulse rate down. To cool down, you can do any activity, such as dribbling a football or jogging, while reducing the speed and intensity. The idea is to keep moving and **gradually slow down** rather than stopping suddenly.

Then repeat the stretches from step 2, but hold them for 15–20 seconds each.

For more information on common injuries see
www.oncampwithkelly.co.uk

Did you know?

- You can **pull a muscle** if your body is not warmed up enough to cope with the demands of the exercise
- You can get **a stitch** if you have eaten or drunk too much before exercise
- **Cramp** in a muscle can result from dehydration or not warming up properly before you exercise

Achilles tendon

The Achilles tendon goes from the calf muscles to the heel bone and it is this tendon that lifts the heel.

Minor damage to the Achilles tendon can be caused by overexercising, a poor running technique or unsuitable footwear. This can inflame the tendon and/or tear the fibres. Most cases clear up with rest and physiotherapy.

If the Achilles tendon is stretched violently – in a bad football tackle, for example – it can snap. This is very painful. It may need an operation or you may have to wear a plaster cast for several weeks.

Body crossword for kids

Across

2) Before exercising you should warm up and afterwards you should _ _ _ _ down

6) What is the one word for all the bones in your body?

7) What parts of your body does air go into when you breathe in?

Down

1) What is the name of the places on your body where you can bend?

3) Your heart is a kind of _ _ _ _ _ _ that sends blood around your body

4) Your heart beats faster when you do this

5) What does your body turn food into?

See page 143 for the answers.

Break the bad news about sugar to your kids

Sorry, kids – but if you eat a lot of sugar, especially if you often have sugary snacks and drinks, you're likely to end up with holes in your teeth.

We all have bacteria in our mouths that love to feast on the sugary snacks and drinks that pass by our teeth. As they feed, the bacteria give out chemicals that dissolve the white coating on teeth.

Brushing your teeth twice a day can help to sweep the bacteria away. And cutting back on sugary snacks and drinks can starve them into submission.

Kelly's fitness challenge for older children

- Older children and teenagers could do this twice a week to increase their fitness, and maybe combine it with a bike ride.

- They can set themselves a target and fill in the chart opposite to record their progress as they increase the number of each exercise they can do.

- To add an element of competition, challenge a friend and see who makes the most progress.

- REMEMBER: WARM UP FIRST – see page 98.

Activity	How many can you do? record your progress at each session				
Sit-ups					
Star jumps					
Step-ups (for 30 seconds)					
Run up and down the stairs (for two minutes)					
Skip without stopping					

Asthma

I had asthma attacks and used inhalers all the way through my childhood. I learned to deal with it. I got short of breath sometimes but it didn't put me off doing sport.

Some children lose their symptoms as they grow up and some find their symptoms become milder. I grew out of asthma at the age of sixteen.

In most cases exercise doesn't make asthma worse, so it shouldn't stop kids exercising.

According to Asthma UK, around one-third of children with asthma miss out on PE and sports about once a week because of their condition. But in fact most should be able to take part as long as their asthma is under control.

Here are Asthma UK's tips to encourage children with asthma to take part in sports and physical activities:

- Make sure your teacher or instructor knows you have asthma
- Increase your fitness levels gradually
- Always have your reliever inhaler with you when you exercise
- If exercise triggers your asthma, use your reliever inhaler immediately before you warm up
- Ensure you always warm up and cool down
- Try to avoid things that trigger your asthma
- If you have asthma symptoms when you exercise, take your reliever inhaler and wait five minutes before starting again

It's also a good idea to provide the school with a spare reliever inhaler (labelled with your child's name) in case your child forgets to take their own.

More information and guides for parents and children can be found at www.asthma.org.uk.

Chapter 7
Looking ahead: Adolescents and sport

I've worked with a lot of children over the years, and I realise how complex teenagers' lives are. Inspiring them to take up a new challenge in sport when they are at an age when there are many distractions can be hard, but actually they just want to be heard – deep down they care as much about their bodies as you do.

This chapter looks at older children and teenagers – especially girls who are more likely than boys to lose interest in sport – and how to keep their enthusiasm alive.

The last two or three years of primary school is the time when children often get hooked on something and start to enjoy it more. There are more clubs, sports and out-of-school activities available to them at this age, too.

Your kids probably spend most of the day sitting down in school – and computers are now such a big thing in their lives. I believe it is really important to get kids out and about, encourage them, tell them to give things a go. Everyone is good at something. They may not all be sports champions, but it's about their ability to make the best of what they've got.

The benefits are immense:
- Fitness
- Weight
- Taking up a healthy lifestyle
- Confidence
- Self-esteem
- Social skills

And at secondary school, they start making choices at twelve or thirteen, so they need to know what they enjoy.

The teenage years

If your child is a pre-teen, chances are you are waiting for the teenage years with a sense of apprehension. The challenges you may have to look forward to include mood swings; lack of motivation for school work; obsessing about physical appearance and clothes; and shyness and lack of self-confidence outside the home, contrasting with stroppiness within. Not to mention a horrendously untidy bedroom and a propensity for door-slamming!

However . . . teenagers are all different. And much of the time, even the really difficult ones can be delightful when caught at the right moment!

Keeping young people motivated to do physical activity in adolescence isn't always easy. This is a time when they sometimes lose interest in things they used to enjoy, become particularly conscious of their body image, and are hypersensitive about what's cool and what's not.

Their bodies, minds and social relationships are all changing fast. They start making their own decisions – it's harder for parents and teachers to influence them. So that means young people themselves are deciding what to eat, where to go and what to do. And what risks to take.

Teenagers' health problems are often related to their own behaviours – the food they eat, smoking, drinking, sex. Keeping them on a healthy, positive track is really important.

The year I was fifteen – after doing well in schools and junior championships in the previous two years – I had a bit of a blip. For some reason, I found it increasingly difficult to train and race. My motivation was lacking. It may just have been that I was fifteen and, like most teenagers, had become curious about discos and was spending some time trying to make a bit of money for myself as well.

I believe sport and physical activity can really help kids through these difficult years. You can combat behavioural problems by getting kids to focus on something like a sport they love.

Sport has been shown to decrease behaviour problems in youngsters – when you're bored, your mind can do anything and kids can end up thinking too much about the wrong things. But if they are involved in sport, they are not bored and they don't have time to get up to mischief.

Schools are trying harder to engage young people in sport and physical activity – they are offering a wider range of activities to appeal to non-sporty pupils as well as those who already love sport. There are special initiatives like the Girls in Sport programme and sports leadership programmes (see below).

And it's brilliant if you can find out-of-school clubs and sports that your teenagers will get involved in and feel passionate about.

If you've got a teenager who doesn't feel like doing anything and can't work up enthusiasm for any kind of sport, try them with the list on page 124.

How bodies change at puberty

It's not only children's mindset that changes with adolescence – their bodies are changing alarmingly too.

Anyone who coaches children and young people in sport needs to understand the effect that puberty and physical development can have on their performance.

In adolescent boys, their height and weight increase quite quickly, their shoulders get broader and they develop more muscle. On average the growth spurt reaches a peak around the age of fourteen, though it can start as early as twelve or as late as fifteen.

Adolescent girls get taller before they get heavier. Their hips usually broaden, which tends to change their running action. For girls, the growth spurt reaches its peak much earlier – on average around twelve, though it may come as early as ten or as late as fourteen.

Compared with girls, adolescent boys develop a greater proportion of bone and muscle relative to fat – so their bodies pack more weight per cubic centimetre than girls.

Younger girls and boys can play alongside one another quite happily, but after puberty boys are bulkier and stronger, so they should not be involved with girls in any sport where this would give them an unfair advantage.

The power of sport for teenagers

Living For Sport uses the power of sport to get young people to feel more positive about school.

It's an initiative for eleven-to sixteen-year-olds that aims to improve their attitudes and behaviour. Students work with their teachers and support staff to set personal targets and goals. After taking part in a range of activities such as sailing, archery and martial arts, they go on to organise a sporting event for a local school or community group.

At the end there's a celebration event, recognising and rewarding the young people's achievements.

Developed by the Youth Sport Trust with BSkyB and the Department for Education and Skills (DfES), Living For Sport is available to all schools.

See www.youthsporttrust.org for more details.

Girls and sport

Girls and sport: why the problem?

Some teenage girls will do ANYTHING to get out of doing PE at school!

There are many reasons why girls are more likely than boys to lost interest in physical activity and sport. These range from issues about their body and self-image to low self-esteem, fear of developing a muscular body, worries about being no good at sport, a feeling that sport isn't 'cool' and even a dislike of their PE kit!

Lots of experts and teachers have been concerned for a long time about the way so many adolescent girls drop out of sport and physical activity. It's something I feel really strongly about too.

I want to help prevent the 40 per cent of girls dropping out of all sports activity by the time they are eighteen and get the 67 per cent of girls who would like to do more exercise than they currently do more active!

Girls Active

As the National School Sport Champion I want to make a real difference in the approach to and delivery of physical activity and sporting opportunities for all young people, but in particular girls. I want to help motivate and inspire them to get involved and stay involved, particularly into their teens and beyond.

GirlsActive is an initiative set up by the Youth Sports Trust and Norwich Union. I go into schools and we do things like street dance, climbing, abseiling and balance work. I work with girls of thirteen to sixteen who have switched off as far as PE and sport go.

At first there are always a lot of tears. The girls have a fear of the unknown, of showing themselves up. They say things like, 'I really can't do it' but I always reply, 'Unless you try, you don't know.' I try to get them past that sense of inability.

But the changes in them as a result of this programme are amazing! When the girls were asked what they had learned about themselves from the initiative, responses ranged from, 'I can do anything if I believe I can' to, 'It's always best to have a go and overcome my fears'. I get them to try things that they said they couldn't do, and in the end their determination to overcome their fears gives them a tremendous sense of accomplishment.

The girls also left some really positive messages on a 'graffiti wall':

- 'Thanks for making PE fun today'
- 'Thanks for this great experience! I've made new friends and started to take part more. Girls need to be valued as much as boys in sport!'
- 'Meeting Kelly Holmes was great. She is an inspiration to many and one day I hope to be as successful as her and compete in the 2012 Olympics. Thank you, Kelly!'
- 'I loved the dance, me and my friend are going to start going every Friday, thanks for showing me something I really like and can keep going to.'

Remember – your mind will talk you out of anything if you let it.

It's easy for teenage girls to get embarrassed – they have issues about body image, they feel intimidated, they lack confidence.

By doing what we did with them, we gave them a boost, made them believe they could do it. That sense of achievement really changed them. And when some of the ones who were really scared showed that they could achieve, the others decided to give it a go too. We gave them opportunities and a voice.

As a result of the Girls Active programme, the girls who participated were more willing to take part in activities, took more pride in their sporting participation and success and were more enthusiastic and motivated. Even their behaviour and general attitude improved.

As more schools take these messages on board, more girls will benefit from sport and physical activity improving their health, fitness and quality of life for years to come. That has to be good news!

Research indicates that physical activity need not be strenuous to achieve real health benefits and reduce the risks of developing coronary heart disease, hypertension, colon cancer and diabetes. Moreover, regular physical activity can reduce symptoms of depression and anxiety, help control weight and help build and maintain healthy bones, muscles and joints.

Girls in Sport, Monitoring and Evaluation: Final Report, Institute of Youth Sport, Loughborough University

My family were quite sporty, but I had my own drive and determination to take things to another level. I got into athletics at twelve and that gave me the focus for the rest of my life.

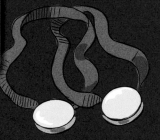

If you want to know more about the issue of women and sport, see the Women's Sports Foundation website, www.wsf.org.uk.

For examples of projects that have increased women's and girls' participation, see www.whatworksforwomen.org.uk.

Sports leadership for young people

Young people at secondary school can do sports leadership courses and learn about coaching and umpiring, so they can then use these skills with primary school kids.

When these fourteen and fifteen-year-olds are teaching younger children, they get huge respect from them. The older kids learn to speak in front of a group. They act as role models for the younger ones. It is great for their confidence and self-esteem.

Here are some of the initiatives that get secondary school pupils into sports volunteering. By taking part in one of these schemes, they will develop the skills they need to assist teachers, coaches and community-group leaders with sports clubs and events.

Step Into Sport Volunteer Project

Step Into Sport is a project to encourage young people aged fourteen to nineteen to get involved in sports leadership and volunteering and is great for schools, school sport partnerships, students, sports clubs and community organisations.

Participants engage in a programme of sport education at school and take a nationally recognised Sports Leader Award. They then go on to gain practical experience through planning and running a sports festival for primary school children (see www. youthsporttrust.org.uk). They also undertake 'community sports leadership' and 'sport-specific leadership' training, and finally, supported by a teacher mentor, volunteer in sports in their local community.

The national governing bodies of a number of different sports have developed courses specific to their sport, aimed at training and developing the next generation of sports volunteers.

In its first four years, Step Into Sport has trained over 120,000 young people in various leadership awards.

Sports Leaders UK Awards

Many of the young people involved in the Step Into Sport project will work towards the Sports Leaders UK Awards:

- Junior (14 to 16 year olds) Level 1 in Sports Leadership
- Community Sports Leader (16 to 19 year olds) Level 1 in Community Sports Leadership

They do this in Key Stage 4/5 school PE. These programmes develop their ability to organise sport and recreation. See www.bst.org.uk/awards.html for more details.

Sport in secondary schools isn't about shivering on the hockey field any more. And it isn't all about being the best. Schools are still doing the traditional sports but they are doing new activities alongside them – so there is a bigger range of fun opportunities to suit more young people.

Kelly's challenge to teenagers

- Plan a safe cycle route and get your mates to go out with you on your bikes. Take a picnic!
- Plan a challenge for you and your mates – go to the swimming pool and see if you can swim fifty lengths between you
- Plan a hike – your local council's leisure department should have some maps of circular walks in your local countryside
- Plan an orienteering challenge or treasure hunt for your mates

Teens: plan an orienteering challenge!

- Plan a route in a wood, fields or open space.
- Put questions or letters at strategic points around the route – players have to visit each place to find them.
- Write down instructions on how to get around the route from each point to the next. Indicate where the clues are (e.g. 'Go down the side of the field until you reach the tree. Write down the number you can see on the tree. Turn left and continue to the fence,' etc.).
- Players set off in pairs, with an instruction sheet and a pen or pencil.
- Leave a short interval between each pair setting off.
- Pairs go round the route, visiting all the points and writing down the letter or number or the answer to the question.
- At the end, players have to solve an anagram, using the letters they have collected. Or check which pair got the answers to all the questions.

Safety points

- Every pair of players should have a whistle or personal alarm and/or mobile phone just in case of emergencies
- Check with your parent or carer before you start organising the challenge to make sure it's OK with them
- Make sure everyone's parents or carers know where they are going and what time to expect them back
- If players are planning to run round the course, get them to do a warm-up first and a cool-down afterwards (see page 98)

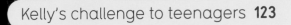

Something for everyone

A teenage girl once said to me: 'I don't like any kind of sport.' And I said: 'Come back to me when you've tried a hundred different sports!'

If your child says the same thing, give them this list. Ask them to consider each activity and give it one of these ratings:

- ⊙ Yes, I'd like to try it if possible
- ⊙ No, I don't fancy it
- ⊙ Maybe – I'd give it a whirl

There's a physical activity out there for everyone. It's just a case of finding your niche!

ACTIVITY	Yes, no or maybe? Indicate with ✓ x or ? in the box		
		Cycling	☐
		Diving	☐
		Football	☐
		Girls' football	☐
		Girls' rugby	☐
Abseiling	☐	Golf	☐
Aerobics	☐	Gymnastics	☐
African dance	☐	Hiking	☐
Aqua aerobics	☐	Hockey	☐
Archery	☐	Horse-riding	☐
Badminton	☐	Irish dancing	☐
Basketball	☐	Jive	☐
Belly dancing	☐	Jogging	☐
Bhangra dance	☐	Judo	☐
Boccia	☐	Juggling	☐
Bollywood dance	☐	Karate	☐
Bowling	☐	Line dancing	☐
Boxercise	☐	Martial arts	☐
Boxing	☐	Morris dancing	☐
Canoeing	☐	Netball	☐
Cheerleading	☐	Orienteering	☐
Circuit training	☐	Paddlesport	☐
Circus skills	☐	Power walking	☐
Climbing	☐	Rambling	☐
Country dancing	☐	Refereeing	☐
Cricket	☐	Rowing	☐
Curling	☐	Rugby League	☐

Rugby Union	☐
Running	☐
Sailing	☐
Salsa	☐
Skateboarding	☐
Ski slopes (indoor)	☐
Skipping	☐
Squash	☐
Street dance	☐
Surfing	☐
Swimming	☐
Synchronised swimming	☐
Table tennis	☐
Tai Chi	☐
Tennis	☐
Ten-pin bowling	☐
Trampolining	☐
Water polo	☐
Yoga	☐

- Try the leisure and recreation department at your local council
- Phone local community centres, leisure centres, the library
- Check websites for national governing bodies of the various sports, which may be able to tell you about local clubs (see page 142).
- Do a search on the Internet to find the nearest place to you that offers a particular sport or activity

Of course, not all of the activities listed here require an organised club or class – with some, you can just get on with it, either with friends or on your own.

If you do need a club then, obviously, what's on offer depends on where you live. Once you know the kind of activities that appeal to your son or daughter, you can check out which ones are available locally:

I've always been interested in martial arts, ever since I was a kid. It combines skills, strength and self-defence and gets rid of aggression in a controlled manner. I got my blue belt, competing in army and civilian competitions, and eventually winning the Army Judo Championship.

Top sports website

The BBC has a great website with information about all kinds of sports – from American football and badminton to table tennis, triathlon and weightlifting. There are even video masterclasses on improving your performance – everything from perfecting your swimming strokes to how to swerve past the opposition on the rugby field.

See www.news.bbc.co.uk/sport1/hi/academy for more details.

Youth organisations – providing the challenge teens need

Teenagers are often drawn to taking risks – and for some, that can mean antisocial or potentially self-destructive behaviour. It's the only way they know to get their kicks.

What young people need is the chance to test themselves, but as safely as possible and in a positive way. Sport offers that for some kids. Others get it from their involvement in a youth group like the Scouts or Guides (Rangers and Explorers for older teens) or a scheme like the Duke of Edinburgh Award.

'I belonged to the Brownies and then the Girl Guides. The thing I liked most about being a Guide was the camping, making fires and living outdoors. Putting up the tents, sleeping squashed together in our sleeping bags on the bumpy ground, cooking marshmallows on the campfire and singing songs was my idea of heaven.

'I loved all the challenges we were set, especially crossing the "swamp" on a tightrope. Loads of girls fell in but I'd hang on for dear life, determined not to.'

If your child isn't into sports, being part of an organisation like the Scouts or Guides (or Rangers or Explorers) can provide lots of physical activity, both indoors and outdoors. They learn new skills and get the chance to try challenges on their own and without their parents' help – which helps develop a sense of responsibility and independence.

Most Scouts, Guides, Rangers and Explorers get to do exciting stuff like hiking, camping and 'wide games' – which involve lots of running around fields and open spaces – sometimes in pitch darkness! Belonging to a youth group, with trained and experienced leaders, exciting activities and a great social life, can really enhance young people's lives. I loved being in the Guides.

In the Duke of Edinburgh Award scheme – which many schools offer – as well as outdoor expeditions, young people learn new skills or hobbies and do some voluntary work in their community. The scheme is made up of three levels – bronze, silver and gold – each designed to challenge youngsters. It is open to kids aged from fourteen to seventeen.

I found the sense of challenge I was looking for by enrolling in the Duke of Edinburgh's Award Scheme. 'Train, plan and complete an adventurous journey in the countryside' was one of the categories we had to enter for our bronze badge. My friend Kerrie's dad dumped her, me and two other friends in Shipbourne, Kent, laden down with our backpacks, bedrolls and a tent. We'd been given a map and a compass and told to find the local church, then make our way to the campsite at Stansted. We got hopelessly lost and ended up huddled together under the trees in the pouring rain, nibbling our Kendal mint cake, waiting to be rescued!

Chapter 8
Going further in sport

If your child has the potential to do well in or loves a particular sport, then you might want to find them a local sports club. There, your child will meet coaches who are qualified to help them improve their skills and go further in their chosen sport.

At secondary school, because I was good at running, my PE teacher suggested I join Tonbridge Athletics Club. I remember my mum driving me there for the first time. My poor mother's heart must have been sinking at the thought of ferrying me to yet another activity, after the ones I had already tried and given up. However, I was looking forward to going there. I took no notice of Mum's veiled threat: 'Well, you'd better stick at this one.' Little did we know!

This chapter tells you a little about sports clubs and coaching and how they can help children and young people progress in sport. It also looks at how you can support your child. There are so many opportunities and so much advice out there that there should be no excuses!

The coach's job is to get the best out of your child

You will learn whether your child has the potential to go further in the sport – if that is what they want. You'll also quickly find out how the system works in terms of leagues, competitions and so on.

In professional sport, it's all about winning. But in youth sports, the emphasis is different – or it should be. As well as winning, getting involved more seriously in a sport means young people learn about:

- Always trying their best
- Continuing to learn and improve
- Learning from mistakes
- Not being afraid to make mistakes – or to lose
- Responsibility
- Teamwork
- Fair play
- Setting and working towards goals
- Leadership
- Persevering when things don't work out
- Motivation
- Ability to concentrate and focus
- Confidence and self-esteem

The quality of adult leadership is so important in maximising all the positive effects of sport. That's why good coaches and club leaders are vital.

Dave, my coach, always said that he saw something totally different in me as soon as he met me. I loved pushing myself towards the targets he set and the feeling of achievement when I met them.

Some children feel they can't do anything. But you just need to say, 'try again' or 'let's see what else you can do'. Inside, your child is still hoping they can do it and they need someone to tell them that they can.

Talk to them about a time you failed at something and tried again.

What to look for in a sports club

If you are leaving your child in the care of a sports club and its leaders, you will want to check it out thoroughly beforehand. A well-run club will be happy to answer your questions about their activities and policies.

Check that the leader or coach:

- Has a recognised certificate or qualification – as well as sports skills, they should have been trained in child protection and health and safety procedures
- Has had a Criminal Record check (see Child Protection, page 133)
- Is running the activity as part of a recognised organisation, such as a sports club or charitable or voluntary organisation

What's involved?

- Find out what the training and coaching sessions will involve.
- Ask the coach what he or she hopes to achieve.
- Find out how often the training sessions are held and how often there are matches and competitions to go to.
- Ask about leagues and tournaments the teams play in – this could affect how often and how far you are going to need to drive your child to get to matches.
- Find out what costs will be involved – e.g. kit, transport, session fees. For away fixtures and other events, the sports club or centre should tell you about the arrangements, including transport to and from the venue. You should also be given information about the venue itself. If it is a long way from home, you should be given a contact number for use in emergencies.
- What is the ratio of leaders to children/young people? Ratios should be based on the age of the children involved, the degree of risk and whether the children have disability needs. The younger the participants, the more supervision is needed. If the activity is mixed gender, male and female staff should be available.
- Supervision: There should be someone in charge to supervise staff and volunteers at all times.

- Health and safety: a leader should be qualified in first aid. There should also be a first-aid box and arrangements for drinks. There should be guidelines about dealing with injuries. The premises should satisfy fire regulations.
- Your child's personal care needs: if your child needs help with using the toilet, feeding or medication, ask how this will be done.
- If your child or you have any worries, who can you talk to? The sports organisation should be prepared to listen and tell you what to do.
- Does the organisation have a child protection policy? You should be able to see it if you ask.
- What boundaries exist concerning club relationships? The club should have clear guidelines about physical contact and social activities between staff, volunteers, participating children and parents.
- There should be a written code of behaviour showing what is required of staff, volunteers and participants. Avoid organisations that permit bullying, shouting, racism, sexism or any other kind of oppressive behaviour.

Always provide the club with an alternative contact name or number so that, in an emergency, they can get in touch when you are not available on your usual number.

The Child Protection in Sport Unit has lots of useful information that parents should know (see www.thecpsu.org.uk).

Look for a club where all the coaches are checked with the Criminal Records Bureau – this is a check to ensure they have not committed an offence that would make them unsuitable to work with children and young people. All established clubs should carry out CRB checks on their leaders and coaches – and ideally their volunteers as well.

However, CRB clearance only goes so far. It only picks up people who have actually been caught. Clubs should also have a child protection policy and clear guidelines and safeguards.

Keeping kids safe

No parent wants their child to be distressed in any way, ever. But sport, just like any other profession, has a few people in it who are capable of doing harm.

Very occasionally, certain kinds of physical, emotional or sexual mistreatment or lack of care can happen within sports clubs. For instance:

- Forcing a child into training and competition that exceeds the capacity of his or her immature and growing body; or giving drugs to enhance performance or delay puberty.
- Subjecting children to constant criticism, name-calling, sarcasm or bullying. Putting them under consistent pressure to perform to unrealistically high standards is also a form of emotional abuse. Bullying by adults can harm children both physically and emotionally. Bullying can include deliberately embarrassing or humiliating a child, treating them unfairly or verbally abusing them, or deliberately ignoring them.
- Sexual abuse – coaching techniques that involve physical contact with children could potentially create situations where sexual abuse may go unnoticed.
- Exposing children to undue cold or heat, or to unnecessary risk of injury.

Young disabled children

Some disabled children and young people are mentally or physically more vulnerable than others, which could make it easier for abusers to exploit them. They may also find it more difficult to recognise and report abuse, and to be believed.

School-club links

More and more schools are making links with local sports clubs, so that children and young people can make a smooth and easy transition from school to club sport.

The idea is that these sports clubs provide a welcoming environment for young people, so that more young people go on to join the clubs – whether it's just for fun or whether they are aiming for serious sporting success.

Some clubs hold taster days, provide coaching in schools or run after-school clubs, to get young people interested in their sport.

Who is involved?

- PE teachers from schools
- Coaches, assistants and volunteers from local sports clubs
- School sport partnerships (see page 66), local authorities' sport development units and sports national governing bodies also sometimes help set up links

> **'People involved in school-club links need to be committed, enthusiastic and act as positive role models.'**
>
> *School-club links*, Department for Education and Skills

Of course, schools want to know that any sports clubs they work with are high quality and adopt good practice when working with children and young people. That's where Clubmark comes in.

Clubmark is an award given by Sport England to **high-quality clubs with junior sections**. Clubs get this accreditation because they have adopted good practice and are providing a safe and effective environment for young people.

Is this club the right one for your child?

If you are deciding whether a particular club will suit your child, then as well as all the points above, you will need to look at the culture within the club:

- Is the focus purely on winning and losing or will it suit children who want to play for fun?
- Will your child get a chance to play in matches even if they're not a star player?
- Do the coaches seem to be on the children's wavelength?
- Are they positive, encouraging rather than criticising?

Here are some comments from parents:

- 'My son got disenchanted with his football club – the coach always put out the best players in matches. There are places like academies and schools of excellence for special youngsters that they can go to if they are good enough. But this was just an ordinary football club for youngsters that he wanted to be part of – and it was being run on the basis that "we must win at all costs". Even some parents agreed with that – but I don't.'
- 'For one whole winter, we had to drive to Surrey every three weeks because the club had joined the Surrey league. It took us an hour and a half to get there and even longer to get back. Apparently there wasn't an under-thirteens league any nearer. You have to go where the games are – and it is quite a big commitment.'
- 'In our club, in a lot of matches, the manager makes sure the players at the bottom of the list have the chance to play too.'
- 'Our Sundays are all spoken for now, but we don't mind. It's a very important part of his life – and we enjoy it too. For parents, the social side is great.'

Finding clubs for young disabled people

The route into a club for a young disabled person may be slightly different and will need to be researched carefully. There are specialist sports for disabled people; boccia, goalball, seated volleyball, for example, and then there are a whole set of Paralympic sports.

School sport partnerships are setting up multi-sport clubs for young disabled people to give them more opportunities, but also to help identify talented young people and help them on their way. These multi-sport clubs are probably the best start for any disabled child. Once in them the experts around them will help them find their best route to carry on in sport.

The Youth Sport Trust has developed, in partnership with EFDS, a website to support young people in sport. You can find it at www.youthsporttrust.org/inclusion.

Developing young athletes

'Long-term athlete development' is a staged approach to training and competition that maximises a young person's potential. The main aim is to produce more sportspeople who can achieve at the highest levels – but it also enables coaches to encourage and support people at every level to fulfil their own potential.

Quite a few sports have developed their own plans for 'long-term athlete development' – you can find these on www.sportscoachuk.org.

When your child needs encouragement

There will be times when your child is feeling negative or disappointed because they didn't get on the team. It's hard for children to be told they are not good enough. They need all the encouragement parents can give, so they will keep trying and keep going.

On the other hand, if your child is not happy there any more, you need to listen and take that on board. If a child says, 'I don't feel like going,' it's a sure sign they are not enjoying it.

Encouragement and pushing are two different things. Encouragement is when you want them to do it because they are enjoying it. Pushing can turn a child off.

When I was growing up there were a lot of kids who were better than me. But unlike me, they never made the transition to senior, because they were pushed too hard.

I can imagine now how some parents are pushing their children in the hope they will get to the 2012 Olympics . . .

Are you a model sports parent?

Try our quiz (but please don't take it too seriously!)

A. How dedicated are you?

- ☐ Are you prepared to spend your Sunday morning on the touchlines, cheering, rather than having breakfast in bed with the newspaper?
- ☐ Would you think nothing of driving for two hours plus, every weekend, to get them to a match?
- ☐ Are you happy to spend your Easter holiday staying in a random windswept caravan park so your child can take part in the hockey festival?
- ☐ Do you wash muddy kit week after week without grumbling?

B. How supportive are you?

- ☐ Are you happy if they enjoy their sport, regardless of how well they do in matches and competition?
- ☐ Do you think your approval is important to your child?
- ☐ Do you tell your child you know they tried hard, even if they and/or their team didn't win?
- ☐ Do you tell them you are proud of them – often?
- ☐ Do you find things to praise – like the way they turn out for training in the cold and wet, week after week – even when they aren't performing so well?
- ☐ Do you help them check they have everything they need – kit, food, drinks – before setting off?

C. Are you a credit to the sports club?

- ☐ Do you know the names of the leaders?
- ☐ Do you always arrive on time before and after your child's activity?
- ☐ Do you always tell the club if your child can't attend a planned activity or if you need to make changes in pick-up arrangements?
- ☐ Do you actively support the club's activities?

D. You're not a pushy parent – are you?

- ☐ Do you steer your child away from sports you wouldn't want them to do?
- ☐ Do you direct them towards your own favourite sport?
- ☐ Does your child feel they would not be allowed to give up even if they wanted to?
- ☐ After a match, do you tell your child how you think they did, rather than asking them what they think?
- ☐ Do you explain to them all the things they did wrong in the match?
- ☐ Do you see your child as a future Olympic champion?
- ☐ Do you want them to be the best – at all costs?

E. Are you setting a good example?

- ☐ Have you ever sworn at a referee (even under your breath)?
- ☐ Have you ever argued with another parent on the touchlines (even though they were clearly in the wrong)?
- ☐ If your child's team loses, do you complain all the way home?
- ☐ Has a club official ever asked you to keep quiet or – the shame! – even to leave?

I'm quite sure you scored all YES answers in A, B and C – and all NO answers in D and E . . . and that makes you a model sports parent.

Congratulations!

A keen tennis player in the family?

www.britishtennisparents.com is a website for parents of junior tennis players, developed by Judy Murray – tennis coach and mother of tennis players Jamie and Andy.

It's full of useful tips on training, coaching, tournaments and so on, and answers some of the questions parents ask, such as:

- How can I get my child involved in tennis?
- How do I know if my local club is good?
- How do I maximise my child's potential?
- How much should my child practice?

Talented athletes

There are national performance camps for elite young athletes. www.talentladder.org is a web-based resource for teachers, coaches and parents and national support network for talented young disabled athletes. You can also visit my website www.doublegold.co.uk/talentedathletes.

Getting involved

As well as being a supportive parent and cheering on the team, you might want to go one step further and get involved yourself. There are lots of ways you could do this – from providing transport and helping with refreshments and training sessions to training as a coach, manager or referee.

Weigh up whether you have the time to spare and can make the commitment.

You'll also want to consider how your child will feel if you are around all the time while they are at the sports club. For some young people, playing sport and going to matches without parents in tow makes them feel grown-up. Involvement in a club is a good way for young people to develop a sense of independence from home and family. So make sure your child will welcome your presence before you promise to help with training sessions!

Interested in coaching?

Coaching children and young people can be really satisfying and rewarding.

There are lots of coaching courses available for different sports and activities – see the website of the national governing body for the sport you're interested in.

For a good introduction, read *How to Coach Children in Sport* (published by sports coach UK). Also, sports coach UK runs workshops in 'Coaching Children and Young People' and 'Good Practice and Child Protection'.

See the website www.sportscoachuk.org or email bsc@sportscoachuk.org for more information.

Mentoring the high-fliers

In January 2004, as I prepared for the Athens Olympics, I realised that – whatever happened at the Games – I wanted to help young athletes learn what it takes to become world class and to achieve their dreams. I believed that athletes could learn from my life, with its mixture of successes, setbacks and disappointments. I hoped I could help them develop in their own careers.

I approached Norwich Union about the idea and they were keen to fund the initiative – On Camp with Kelly was born!

Then the unthinkable happened and I won TWO gold medals at the Athens Olympics in August 2004. But despite the huge changes to my life following the Games, I was still completely committed to On Camp with Kelly. In the last three years, nearly forty young British female endurance athletes have been involved in On Camp with Kelly and have attended get-together weekends around the UK and training camps in South Africa, Spain and Australia.

The young athletes have benefited from grants and top-class medical support as well as my advice and mentoring.

I plan to make On Camp with Kelly bigger and better, with the backing of Norwich Union, through to 2012 and beyond.

For more information, see my website: www.doublegold.co.uk/ocwk/.

And finally . . .

I am living proof that dreams can come true. As I have said so many times: never put less than a hundred per cent into what you want to do. At least then, like me, you will never live with regrets.

WANT TO FIND OUT MORE?

SPORT AND ACTIVITY

My website is full of information about my work with schools, athletes, adults, charities, initiatives and regular competitions.

Visit www.doublegold.co.uk for more information.

Youth Sport Trust

The Youth Sport Trust works in close partnership with schools and sport to provide quality physical education programmes for children and young people aged from eighteen months to eighteen years. The Youth Sport Trust's TOPS programme provide a series of linked and progressive schemes for young people and delivers training and adapted equipment for teachers, coaches and sports leaders.

Their website is www.youthsporttrust.org.

Sports Leaders UK

Sports Leaders UK is responsible for the organisation of Sports Leader Awards. See www.sportsleaders.org for more details.

Swimming and water safety website

www.qca.org.uk/safeswimming is aimed at teachers, parents and pupils. It provides practical ideas, resources and guidance to help children and young people learn how to swim safely and well.

Tennis

The website for parents of junior tennis players is www.britishtennisparents.com.

Sporting Equals

This organisation promotes racial equality in sport. See www.sportingequals.com for more details.

sports coach UK

The website of sports coach UK is www.sportscoachuk.org, and contains lots of useful information for anyone involved in sports or fitness coaching – or interested in becoming a coach.

UK Sports Governing Bodies

UK Sport have a comprehensive database of website links and contact details for many of the UK sports governing bodies. Their website is www.uksport.gov.uk/links.asp.

Dragon Sport – Sports Council for Wales

This initiative promotes sporting opportunities for seven to eleven-year-olds in seven modified sports in Welsh primary schools. It is delivered through a network of 'Dragon Sports Co-ordinators'.

Parents can become volunteers, working with teachers and coaches to develop after-school and community sports clubs.

Telephone 029 2030 0500 or see their website at www.dragon-sport.co.uk.

Youth Sport – Sports Council for Northern Ireland

Youth Sport caters for children of all abilities at three levels: neighbourhood, local and district. The focus is on developing opportunities in thirteen sports at schools and in the community. See www.sportni.net for more information.

Coaching qualifications/awards

For a list of relevant awards and qualifications, visit www.bhf.org.uk/youngpeople and select 'downloadable resources' followed by 'useful information'.

British Heart Foundation

The British Heart Foundation produces some excellent resources on heart health and physical activity.

To order any of them, phone 01604 640016 and quote the order code below:

- *Pocket Play Pack* **(7–11-year-olds) G79**
- *Get kids on the go!* **(booklet for parents) G80**
- *Get kids on the go!* **(Welsh/English version) G80/w**
- *Artie Beat club* **(membership form for 7–11) G48B**

Disability sport

English Federation of Disability Sport

Their website www.efds.co.uk has links to a huge number of disability sports organisations, including: British Blind Sport, UK Deaf Sport, English Sports Association for People with Learning Disability, and the British Wheelchair Racing Association.

Scottish Disability Sport

Visit www.scottishdisabilitysport.com.

Disability Sports NI

Visit www.dsni.co.uk.

Sports Disability Cymru

Visit www.disability-sport-cymru.co.uk.

Inclusive Fitness Initiative

This initiative awards the Inclusive Fitness Mark, a quality mark for health clubs, leisure centres, fitness centres in schools, universities, hotels etc. that have accessible facilities, inclusive fitness equipment and staff with the appropriate training and skills. There are now 180 inclusive facilities across England with the IFM quality mark.

For more details see www.inclusivefitness.org.

Halliwick Association of Swimming Therapy

The Halliwick Method teaches water confidence and swimming to children and adults with any kind of disability. See their website – www.halliwick.org.uk – for details of local clubs or how to train as an instructor.

Youth Sport Trust

www.inclusion.youthsporttrust.org.

The Food Standards Agency

This is an independent government department. Its website has practical help on healthy eating and understanding food labelling, including advice on children's diets.

See www.food.gov.uk and www.eatwell.gov.uk for more information.

Children's Food Campaign

The Children's Food Campaign wants to improve young people's health and wellbeing through better food – and food teaching – in schools and by protecting children from junk food marketing.

Visit their website at www.children'sfoodcampaign.org.uk.

School Food Trust

The School Food Trust is an independent organisation set up to make sure school food is healthier. It has lots of advice and information on school food on its website at www.schoolfoodtrust.org.

Answers: Body crossword for kids
Across: 2) cool, 6) skeleton, 7) lungs
Down: 1) joints, 3) muscle, 4) exercise, 5) energy

Index